REFLECTIVE PRACTICE IN COUNSELLING AND PSYCHOTHERAPY

Other books in this series

What is Counselling & Psychotherapy?
by Norman Claringbull ISBN 978 1 84445 361 0

Creating the Therapeutic Relationship in
Counselling and Psychotherapy by Judith Green ISBN 978 1 84445 463 1

Counselling and Psychotherapy in Organisational
Settings by Ruth Roberts and Judy Moore ISBN 978 1 84445 614 7

To order, please contact our distributor: BEBC Distribution, Albion Close, Parkstone, Poole, BH12 3LL. Telephone 0845 230 9000, email: **learningmatters@bebc.co.uk**. You can also find more information on each of these titles and our other learning resources at **www.learningmatters.co.uk**

Want to write for the Counselling and Psychotherapy Practice series? Contact the Commissioning Editor, Luke Block (luke@learningmatters.co.uk), with your ideas and proposals.

REFLECTIVE PRACTICE IN COUNSELLING AND PSYCHOTHERAPY

SOFIE BAGER-CHARLESON

Series editor: Norman Claringbull

LearningMatters

First published in 2010 by Learning Matters Ltd

British Library Cataloguing in Publication Data
A CIP record for this book is available from the British Library.

ISBN: 978 1 84445 360 3

This book is also available in the following ebook formats:

Adobe ebook	ISBN: 978 1 84445 695 6
EPUB ebook	ISBN: 978 1 84445 694 9
Kindle	ISBN: 978 1 84445 988 9

Cover design by Code 5 Design Associates
Project management by Diana Chambers
Typeset by Kelly Winter
Printed and bound in Great Britain by TJ International, Padstow, Cornwall

Learning Matters Ltd
33 Southernhay East
Exeter EX1 1NX
Tel: 01392 215560
info@learningmatters.co.uk
www.learningmatters.co.uk

FSC
Mixed Sources
Product group from well-managed forests and other controlled sources
Cert no. SGS-COC-2482
www.fsc.org
© 1996 Forest Stewardship Council

Contents

Foreword

Modern counsellors and psychotherapists know that reflection is an integral part of everyday therapeutic practice and that an understanding of reflective practice is vital. After all, the talking therapies are essentially self-transforming processes and, therefore, therapists (and their clients) must learn how to critically examine themselves.

Sofie Bager-Charleson has a PhD in Reflective Practice in Education and, as a very experienced therapist, she is an academic supervisor of psychotherapy doctoral candidates at Middlesex University. In this book she offers us her well-crafted ideas about how we can all become much better reflective practitioners by revealing to us what reflective practice is all about and how to do it.

Sofie shows us how to put the 'self' into self-awareness and invites us to experiment with reframing (reinterpreting) our values and our experiences. Put simply, Sofie challenges us to practise what we preach. Do we really work with our clients in ways that are consistent with our theoretical and personal beliefs? Do we really understand ourselves? Could reflective self-awareness help us to become more aware of how our own biases and individual backgrounds impact on how we relate to our clients? Will critical reflexivity show us how we and the wider world are linked together? Dip into this book and you will discover a scholastically sound, but nevertheless very readable, account of these essential therapeutic concepts. Some writers make reflective practice seem a difficult, jargonistic topic but Sofie offers us a user-friendly way through what can sometimes look like a daunting philosophical maze. This is a very 'hands on' book and Sofie also shows us in detail how to put ideas into everyday therapeutic practice.

The benefits of this book are further boosted by the contributions of Dr Biljana van Rijn, Head of Clinical Services at the Metanoia Institute, and Professor Simon du Plock, Director of Metanoia's Psychotherapy Doctoral Program. Sofie and her contributors acknowledge that today's counsellors and psychotherapists are essentially practitioner-researchers and explain that research is a vital tool for all therapists, not just those in academia.

In Chapters 5 and 6, Biljana van Rijn helps us to better understand how research can be understood from a reflective perspective. She shows us how evidence-based practice and reflective practice complement each other and offers an overview of the developments in evidence-based reflective thinking that will assist all practitioner-researchers to better appreciate this vital topic. In Chapter 7, Simon du Plock expands on the value of therapy research to everyday practitioners and he writes about work-based and reflective learning with the particular aim of demystifying research.

A clear illustration of the importance of reflective practice in the ownership of one's own work is shown in the open and honest manner in which Sofie, Biljana and Simon disclose information about themselves and their thinking. This book makes it crystal clear how important it is for anyone interested in the talking therapies to improve their understanding of reflective practice. *Reflective Practice in Counselling and Psychotherapy* is a vital, leading-edge contribution to this process and is an essential component of the Counselling and Psychotherapy Practice Series.

Norman Claringbull
Series Editor

Acknowledgements

I should like to thank the many colleagues, students and clients who have contributed with material, directly and indirectly, to this book. I am particularly indebted to Simon du Plock and Biljana van Rijn, who have contributed separate chapters. They have not only generously shared their special knowledge and expertise but have also been a continuous source of inspiration. There are innumerable others who have made important contributions both recently and over a period of time. I would like to express my gratitude to my supportive editors, Luke Block and Lauren Simpson. I also want to thank my mother, Anna-Lena, for showing such an interest in my work and contributing with interesting angles and perspectives. Finally, I want to seize this opportunity to let my family know how much they mean to me. Dermot and Fina, Finbar and Leo – you bring purpose and meaning to everything I do.

I should like to dedicate this book to my father, Börje, who died three years ago. He taught me the true meaning of viewing the world from different perspectives.

Preface

'OWNING' OUR QUESTIONS

Reflective practice requires the inquirer to 'own' their involvement in a situation, no matter what they investigate or who they engage with professionally. It involves owning one's questions and issues rather than relying on others to 'carry' them for us (Guggenbuhl-Craig, 1991).

There are three contributors to this book, and we have chosen to 'own' our interest in reflective practice in different ways. As the instigator of the book, I have chosen to share some of my reflections here.

A STORY NOT A REPORT

First, it needs to be explained that this book is a story, rather than a report. The term 'story' highlights that the text is 'constructed' (Holloway and Jefferson, 2002) rather than reflecting a pre-existing reality. In their book about qualitative research, Holloway and Jefferson highlight a 'responsibility' for the narrator to be 'clear' about their input:

> *[T]he difference between a story and a report . . . is that in telling a story, the narrator takes responsibility for making the relevance clear . . . the agenda is open to development and change, depending on the narrator's experience. It . . . recognises that the story told is constructed (within the research and the interview context) rather than being a neutral account of a pre-existing reality.*
>
> (Holloway and Jefferson, 2002: 32)

SOFIE'S STORY

Throughout this book I will try to reflect on my own underlying personal, theoretical and cultural motives for reflective practice, and my assumptions around it. What do I need to alert you, the reader, to with regard to my own framing? What can I say about my underlying assumptions and potential blind spots?

It is not only difficult but to some extent impossible to 'know' ourselves well enough as 'knowers' in the sense that reflective practice proposes. It is also, quite frankly, embarrassing. It requires of the practitioner, the researcher or, as is the case here, the author to step down from a comfortable 'know-it-all' place to a sometimes embarrassing and always vulnerable position. Frame reflection involves a shift of power; it admits that the 'knower' has blind spots and puts actions and strategies into a perspective where others can access and assess one's meaning and subsequent decision-making processes. By admitting to our 'framings', we are also saying, 'I may be biased or have a restricted view due to personal, cultural and/or theoretical circumstances and assumptions'. We are admitting to the fact that we may need to have our 'lenses' or 'glasses' checked (Knott and Scraggs, 2008). We open up to critique, admit to prejudices and expect to confront our own underlying personal, cultural and theoretical assumptions.

UNDERLYING CULTURAL ASSUMPTIONS

I was born and raised in Sweden, and both implicit and explicit cultural assumptions 'came alive' to me as I moved abroad, first to Spain and then to England. Recognising how social values change depending on where you live both surprised me and created opportunities for personal development. To be a 'foreigner' involves a certain degree of diplomatic immunity to norms and values. You notice, for example, how others pay attention to unspoken rules that to an outsider may seem pointless or unimportant. It was really only when I lived outside Sweden that I realised how many social norms and collectively held values I had incorporated in my daily life. When I moved abroad I was confronted with different and, at times, contrasting sets of beliefs. My social democratic and Ingmar Bergman-inspired culture was contrasted – and, I must say, beautifully enriched – by the post-Franco-fuelled 'Movida' movement and Almodovar-spiced culture in Spain, where we lived for four years. The entrepreneurial Thatcherism that characterised England during the 1980s came as a shock when I eventually settled in the UK with my British-born husband.

DOMINATING NARRATIVES

I believe that each society surrounds its citizens with 'culturally available building blocks' (Dallos and Miell, 1996) to construct meaning. Language plays an important role when people are learning to make sense of things. The way we talk – or do not talk – about things shapes our thinking about ourselves and the world around us. *Folkbildning* is a Swedish concept that translates roughly into 'education of the people' and sums up what I brought with me in terms of underlying cultural values and assumptions when moving abroad. Folkbildningsrådet, the Swedish National Council of Adult Education, writes about *Folkbildning* in a way that captures the 'discourse' that had become an intrinsic part of my thinking on both a personal and professional level. The *Folkbildning* ethos underpins what Schön would call my 'framing' of social realities:

> *Every year, several million Swedes gather to participate in Swedish liberal adult education, folkbildning. Writing courses, choirs, music, languages, environmental issues . . . Study circles and high school courses are available in hundreds of different subjects. Knowledgeable and active citizens constitute the core of a democratic society . . . Folkbildning's conceptual heritage stretches back more than a century . . . it grew forth in a Sweden where the level of education was low and large groups of the population were excluded from higher education. Folkbildning became the answer to people's longing for knowledge and desire to influence societal development. Still today a central concept is everyone's right to knowledge and development. A society with little educational divide is a central goal of Folkbildning.*

It is important to note that the above text is not a political manifesto but official information about study groups ranging from creative writing to knitting. When I moved to England, I was struck by the difference with which private and public interests were discussed. 'State intervention', for example, means different things in the UK, Spain and Sweden. The mockingly used phrase 'nanny state' is an example of a narrative 'building block' that helps us to understand attitudes towards state involvement within Great Britain. Education and child-rearing, for example, are areas where, in contrast to Sweden, the rights of the individual predominate: attitudes towards independent schooling and smacking remain open to personal choice, and this stunned me at first.

The flip side to a society that prioritises collectivism is a society that lacks tolerance for differences. It is easy to feel like the odd one out in a culture designed for conformity. *Lagom är bäst* is another underpinning concept and assumption that I grew up with. It translates into 'virtue in moderation', and there is a strong sense of social control conveyed in this concept, for good and for bad.

Just how these underlying cultural values shaped my everyday life, privately and professionally, did not occur to me until I moved abroad. I had not considered how my social conscience was something that I had grown up to accept as the *only* stance – a universal truth. Moving to Spain and then to England made me acutely aware of the impact of words. The text about *Folkbildning* above is written in a way that was very familiar to me through schooling and the media. In the UK, this type of text comes across as a party political statement. The post-Franco Spain in which I lived during the late

1980s was even more sensitive to potentially politically loaded discourse. England, Spain and Sweden have, in other words, very different attitudes towards public and private interests.

While appreciating their importance, I nevertheless consider cultural values as one of the most difficult areas to understand. Hawkins and Shohet (2008) illustrate this with a Chinese proverb: 'the last one to know the water is the fish'.

UNDERLYING PERSONAL ASSUMPTIONS

Ironically, while *lagom* – moderation – was something that I embraced wholeheartedly as a Swedish citizen, it was a concept and phenomenon that failed to find its way into our home.

Behind closed doors, my own childhood was heavily influenced by my father's manic depression. It affected all members of the family, and I have no doubt that this prompted me to become a psychotherapist. With some regret I place myself in the category of therapists that Alice Miller (1997: 8) unflatteringly describes as 'narcissistically damaged' – the type of therapist who, Miller suggests, grew up responding unconsciously to the need of the parent in order to gain a sense of existential security. Miller is very critical of wounded people who become therapists. By having been damaged themselves, therapists may indeed be equipped with an acute sensitivity. Miller suggests, however, that the damaged therapist will use the client as a 'mirroring or idealised self-object' to provide empathic and admiring responses that the therapist failed to receive as a child.

The fact that I responded to my parent's need in order to guarantee myself existential security is my 'shadow', my 'wound' or the 'hook' on to which projections easily get caught, again and again. It is, in other words, an area in need of ongoing attention, to be repeatedly examined and challenged, since it will invariably be provoked in my professional life.

It strikes me as undervaluing the reader to expand on the link between my own past to my interest in reflective practice – it seems an obvious one. The notion of reflective practice makes me 'feel safe', and I need to monitor my own need to 'make the world make sense' so that I do not attempt to make you, the reader, fill my personal voids.

KNOWING AND UTILISING OUR VULNERABILITIES

For therapists as well as clients, therapy is a place where shadows can be confronted. Indeed, this has been the case for me, too. Sussman (1992: 118) suggests that the term benevolence often stems from a low self-esteem and a compulsive need to nurture:

> *A compulsive need to nurture and give to others may use an ego-ideal of unselfish giver as a means of raising chronically low self-esteem . . . For many therapists, an attitude of benevolence constitutes an important feature of their ego-ideal. The term refers to the desire to do good to others and is synonymous with kindness, compassion and charitableness . . . Left unanalysed, however, it can contribute to a significant 'blind spot' limiting the therapist's capacity.*

Miller (1997: 19–20) writes about the inner prison to which adults with an abusive or neglected past are confined as a means of protecting themselves from being overtaken by unexpected emotions. She points out that to practise successfully, therapists must first confront their demons:

> *The therapist's sensibility, empathy, responsiveness and powerful 'antennae' indicate that as a child he probably used to fulfil other people's needs and repress his own . . . If we have never consciously lived through this despair and the resulting rage, and have therefore never been able to work fully through it, we will be in danger of transferring this situation, unconsciously, onto our patients.*

Miller admits that a wounded healer may possess 'sensibility, empathy, responsiveness and powerful antennae', but she refers to a good therapist as a therapist who can practise *in spite of* their wounds. Sedgwick (1994: 111–12) offers a more positive outlook on the 'wounded healer'; like many Jungians he suggests that the therapist is valuable *because* of his wounds. This is a school of thought that resonates with the idea of reflective practice. Sedgwick writes:

> *A central point here is that the patient's unconscious contents can be nourished rather than restricted by the analyst's 'wounds'. Accordingly, analysts need not try to eliminate their 'pathology' but know it and utilise it. This does not mean enacting it, but does mean a fluid awareness of new and old shadows as well as concern not to rationalise or project this upon the client.*

Sedgwick's phrase about *knowing and utilising* one's 'pathology' or flaws captures the essence of reflective practice. This stance involves a new relationship with one's pathology, which needs to be abandoned and mourned, and then picked up again and incorporated in a very different, new way. In all reflective practice, there is an element of loss. We must let go of something that we have held on to for a reason; it must be pulled apart and examined – and often 'put back' again. It is reintegrated with a new purpose as Miller illustrated with the 'antennae', which can be useful if not used for the 'wrong' purposes.

CHANGE IS A QUESTION OF LOSS

The two key components in reflective practice are the problem situations that call for reflection in the first place and their accompanying need for change. Roffey-Barentsen and Malthouse (2009: 20) write:

> *As a learner, when reflecting you will encounter change. Change means loss . . . you will have lost an element that made up a part of what you were.*

Managing personal change invariably requires a stage when prior strategies seem wrong, futile or inadequate. To question one's own stance is an important sign that we are able to adopt new perspectives. In my case, being a 'helper' needed to be reassessed; being a helper and a support to my father was a role around which I had built my life. On one level, I recognised the need for helpers to receive help as part of therapeutic training. I surprised myself, however, by resisting the therapy. I was counting the hours until the required training hours were met. This caused a conflict on several levels. Not only did I lose out on valuable help and support but it also undermined my sense of pride in what I did. After all, if I could not experience the value in therapy myself, how could I expect others to? The destructive side to my 'omnipotent helper' symptom is illustrated in the ABC model (Tschudi, cited in Banister et al., 1994 – see Table 0.1). It is a helpful tool when exploring forces that may prevent us from making the changes that we claim to want to make.

The ABC model illustrates how the loss of my old helper role comes at a personal cost both financially through personal therapy, supervision, readings and courses but more importantly in the sense of reappraising my role vis-à-vis others. Losing my old role also puts me in a vulnerable position; I could be let down again and have to re-experience the pain.

THEORETICAL UNDERSTANDING AND 'TRANSFORMATIVE LEARNING'

Reading up on philosophy has helped immensely in putting my own experiences into a wider context. Seeking principles and themes for originally isolated situations is a significant step in reflective practice. The important stage of reflective practice is what Atherton refers to as 'transformative learning'. It is part of the 'knowing and utilising' process, to put it in Sedgwick's terms.

Further on in this book, Professor Simon du Plock illustrates the meaning of putting an isolated problem through systematic inquiry. This invariably involves exploring patterns and themes and brings with it a 'measurable'

A1 Present position	A2 Preferred position
• I always do everything myself	• I would like to rely more on others
B1 Disadvantages of present position • I turn inwardly for help; I risk isolating myself and lose out on valuable connection and intimacy • I turn to drink or food as support rather than people, and risk my health	**B2 Advantages of preferred position** • I will feel more 'part of the world' • Others will take responsibility • I will enjoy being more easygoing • Letting off steam with others will secure good health
C1 Advantages of present position • Not relying on others protects me; only turning to myself puts me in control of events • Helping others puts me in control	**C2 Disadvantages of preferred position** • I will open up to others and make myself vulnerable to their mood swings and projections • Easygoing means letting down my guards • Turning to others for help puts me in debt, may create dependency and trap me (again) and will most probably disappoint me • It hurts too much to be let down (again)
Source: Tschudi, cited in Banister et al. (1994).	

Table 0.1: The ABC model

aspect to the reflection which Biljana helps to explore. Simon approaches the principle referred to here as 'transformative learning' with reference to personal problematic experiences – in his case, the experience of chronic fatigue. He takes us through the journey in which the problem is 'transformed' into useful knowledge, which ultimately is what reflective practice is all about.

FRAMING SITUATIONS

Reflective practice involves considering the 'lenses' through which we perceive the reality around us so that they become part of how we frame situations. My experience is that knowledge and truth are 'constructed', and I adhere to what Weaver (2008) calls critical constructivism, which implies that although there is a real world out there, we create our own understanding of it through experiences. There are a variety of constructivist models. Rosen and Kuelwein (1996: 5) write:

> *[the constructivist models] hold in common [that] they reject the postulate that our mental representations mirror an objective reality . . . meaning and reality are created and not discovered.*

Frank Smith (1985) expands on this outlook in the following way:

> *The human brain is not in direct contact with the world. To perceive the world in the way it does, the brain must construct a theory of what the world is like. The brain is constantly inventing, learning and comprehending.*

The professional implication of 'lenses' involves a less objective, scientific stance in favour of a more holistic approach to practice. The constructivist perception suggests in most cases that there 'is indeed a real world' but that 'we create our own internal representation, our map, of it' (Weaver, 2008: 1). Weaver continues:

> *[Constructivist psychotherapists] work from the principle that there is more than one judgment of the world. There is no kind of absolute authority to whom we can turn to that will provide 'The Answer'. It is a . . . created interpretation.*

With this as a basic, underpinning belief, I approach methods with an open mind. I believe that we can adopt different methods to select material and present our analysis; that there is no one 'true' stance. But whatever method we choose will have an effect on the outcome of our inquiry.

I will explain more about what I mean by hermeneutic inquiry later on in the book, but, in short, hermeneutics allow the inquirer to approach the inquiry with different 'lenses'; we can, for instance, interpret client work, research interviews or literature with a psychoanalytical 'map', with a humanistic orientation or, as we shall see, with a feminist understanding. Hermeneutics imply that no 'map' is better than another, but the inquirer is required to consider the implications that the maps will have on where we go and what we are likely to come across on our way.

It strikes me that personal experiences have a great impact on what modality we choose to work with. My own interpretive map of therapeutic practice is inspired by psychoanalytical thinking. This resonates with my way of conceptualising and thinking cognitively about the world. It has helped to make sense of private experiences and move them into the stage of 'transformative learning' that therapeutic practice requires. To understand this process further, I have co-authored with colleagues from other 'walks of life' a book about why therapists choose to be therapists. In my own case, psychoanalytic thinking resonates with experiences of living with a presented past. Childhood traumas live on, and the ongoing attempt to separate the past from the present is a theme not just in this book but in my life in general. I may well have resonated with a different modality entirely had my life been different from the start.

EMANCIPATORY INTEREST IN REFLECTIVE PRACTICE

Another set of lenses used in this book is tinted by feminist thinking. Being a woman myself obviously informs this interest, but I particularly subscribe my interest in feminist thinking to work-related experiences. Since working with people with eating disorders, I have grown to agree with many feminist thinkers that there is a 'missing chapter' (Chernin, 1994) in therapeutic literature. Chernin, who specialises in eating disorders, points out that we know all about the strong feelings that boys harbour towards their fathers as part of breaking free and growing up but that we know very little about how girls liberate themselves from their mothers and deal with the fear of 'killing off' their mothers by becoming the adult in the relationship. We will address feminist thinking in Chapter 3.

As Bolton (2005) stresses, reflective practice can fall into the trap of becoming mere confession. It is not, however, a question of navel gazing as a practitioner; ultimately it concerns how we explore and utilise experiences with our clients in mind. This involves consideration of personal and theoretical matters, but it also requires cultural and political interests to be taken into account.

Introduction

This book is written with student counsellors and psychotherapists in mind. It is designed to assist you in developing an understanding of the concept of reflective practice and to help you adopt new perspectives on strategies and experiences. We hope to contribute to the debate about how to safeguard a high professional standard for people seeking therapeutic support. Reflective practice is, in this sense, explored as an additional means of assessing efficacy and quality. But the overall aim of the book is to support counsellors and psychotherapists in their daily, often isolated, clinical practice.

As we have seen, reflective practice requires the inquirer to 'own' their issues and questions rather than relying on others to 'carry' them for us. In his book *The power in the helping professions*, Guggenbuhl-Craig (1991) warns us of the 'rescuing trap'. Therapists, teachers, social workers and other people in the 'helping professions', run a risk of 'projecting' illness, weakness or vulnerability on to clients if they identify exclusively with the healer or the helper pole. The 'split archetype', asserts Guggenbuhl-Craig (2009: 83), struggles with the polarity or distinction between illness and health. He 'will no longer see his wounds and potential for illness. He sees sickness only in the client. He objectifies illness, distances himself from his own weakness [and] elevates himself.' It is expected that the philanthropist hopes to gain 'respect for his generosity' (Sussman, 1992). But to actually seriously consider oneself as 'infallible' requires a level of self-deception that will sooner or later lead to 'some very questionable decision'.

It is hoped that this book will:

- support you in considering your own 'lenses'; and
- help you to develop strategies for meeting the ultimate requirements of reflective practice in terms of 'knowing and utilising' flaws and vulnerability affecting your practice.

REFLEXIVE AWARENESS

Reflective practice (Schön, 1983; Bolton, 2005; White et al., 2008) is an approach that encourages a so-called 'reflexive awareness' in both research and professional practice. Reflexivity encourages us to identify and challenge our own underlying assumptions with the theoretical, cultural and psychological positions of others in mind (Alvesson and Skoldeberg, 2000; Finlay and Gough, 2003; Etherington, 2004; Parker, 1994, 2004). Reflexivity implies that we arrive at the closest we can get to an objective account:

> *through an exploration of the ways in which the subjectivity of the researcher [or practitioner] has structured the way [the problem] is defined in the first place.*
>
> (Parker, 1994)

This reflexive thinking of practice is quickly gaining ground in the areas of social and human studies, therapeutic practice included. No longer are practitioners or researchers regarded as detached experts. Finlay and Gough (2003: 5) write that, instead, a practitioner or researcher is:

> *a central figure who actively constructs the collection, selection and interpretation of data . . . Subjectivity in research is transformed from a problem to an opportunity.*

DIFFERENT ANGLES TO OUR FRAMING

We will look at different theories on reflection. Many agree that several types of reflection are required to cope in a professional context today. Kondrat (cited in Gardner, 2008) distinguishes between three 'alternative perspectives on practice' that can be helpful to keep in mind:

- reflective self-awareness;
- reflexive self-awareness;
- critical reflexivity.

Reflective self-awareness involves being aware of our own biases and preferences in our choice of theory and modality. Reflexive self-awareness is a familiar concern for most therapists: countertransference is an example of a core concept in therapeutic thinking that captures what is going on for therapists themselves during their practice. Critical reflexivity involves questioning our relationship to our own culture. It concerns the link between us and our social structure. Gardner (2008: 145) writes:

> *Being 'critical' adds an expectation of exploring practice in the context of the social system in which it operates, looking, for example, at the*

influence of social expectations about such issues as gender or age, class or ethnicity.

Consider the points below and make a list of at least five points for each topic. Brainstorm, think freely and allow your thoughts and their associations to come as they 'wish'.

- Why do you want to work as a counsellor or psychotherapist? Reflect on something from either your own childhood or the more recent past that you are likely to carry with you into the future.
- How would you describe the social environment in which you grew up? Have you had any particular ethnic, religious or other culturally 'tinted' experiences?

IT IS GOOD TO TALK

Counselling and psychotherapy can be difficult to define. One of my tutors once said: 'I never tell people at a party that I am a psychotherapist; it's too hard to describe what I do and the sound of therapy seems to make people uneasy, like I was going to start to read their mind.'

What does this do to us, I wonder? If we spend 20–25 hours a week doing something that we do not feel we can speak freely about, how does this affect us and our practice? Confidentiality aside, one could argue that there ought to be aspects of our work that we, and others, may benefit from airing and discussing. Within the framework of ethical guidelines, reflective practice favours airing mistakes and discussing problems from different angles. With this in mind, a distinct purpose of this book is to hone your communication skills so that they can be used most effectively in practice, in a supervision setting or in a more public way, for example, when giving talks at conferences.

The terms 'reflection', 'reflective practice' and 'reflexivity' are used frequently today, particularly in the areas of education, social work and health care. The meaning of the term 'reflective practice' is by no means clear or obvious, but it can be summarised as the identification of recurring problems with a view to eventually reaching a stage of 'transformative learning' in which problems are put into context. For most counsellors and psychotherapists, personal therapy, supervision, peer support, courses, reading and writing are essential to transformative learning. Further, transformative learning can be described as the final destination of the reflective practice cycle. Simply put, it is the stage at which one can say: 'I'm glad for my mistakes. They have taught me x and brought the awareness of y into my practice.'

OUR 'FRAMED' UNDERSTANDINGS

Reflective practice reminds us that 'one's expertise is a way of looking at something which once was constructed and may be reconstructed' (Schön, 1983). This highlights the impact our own judgements may have on decisions that sometimes are of a life-altering nature for others. This might be a problem that most of us would like to escape from by adhering to clear-cut 'objectively measured' rights and wrongs. However, the underpinning assumption in reflective practice is that social reality is a landscape where natural, scientifically based 'maps' fail to guide us. In today's debate of evidence-based practice, this idea can seem quite controversial. It may sound as if reflective practice opposes evidence, suggesting that 'anything goes'.

Reflective practice holds the epistemological belief that 'a totally objective reality, one that stands apart from the knowing subject, can never fully be known' (Rosen and Kuelwein, 1996: 5). We make 'maps' of reality (Smith, 1985), and it is this map-making that reflective practice highlights and tries to understand. In evidence-based practice, reflexivity is sometimes portrayed as something that we can erase – annihilate altogether. Webber (2008: 3) writes:

> *Evidence-based practice is about considered rather than reflexive action . . . it requires practitioners to consider evidence before making decisions, rather than acting first and reflecting after the event . . . [and] not being influenced by outside pressures.*

The reflective practice approach assumes that practice will always be influenced by the 'human factor'. It approaches habitual or careless actions from another angle and assumes that there are 'risks for inadequacies of the conventional evidence-based practice approach and its potentially very narrow and hierarchical treatment of evidence' (Taylor, 2008: 76). The new epistemological practice, based on the concept of reflective practice, challenges 'the view of practice as the achievements of fixed unambiguous ends using rule-governed [and] off-the-peg solutions of ready-made knowledge' (Taylor, 2008: 78). Reflective practice thus raises the issue of people being complex beings, and Taylor (2008: 78) continues:

> *[Practitioners working with patients] are not the distanced, emotionally involved expert associated with certain reading of the medical model of practice, but rather the emotionally engaged, committed, warm, empathic practitioner attuned to the need and the feelings of the patient.*

Reflective practice is still a work in progress – the approach is at a stage where each of us plays a part in how it will develop. It invites us to consider and explore our practice in new light and, as Hall (1996: 6) suggests, to 'make tacit knowledge explicit'. Schön and Rein (1994: 26) offer the concept 'framing' to highlight the dilemma involved in policy making in today's society:

> *[T]here is no way of perceiving and making sense of social reality except through a frame, for the very task of making sense of complex, information-rich situations requires an operation of selectivity and organisation, which is what 'framing' means.*

Frame reflection sometimes causes us to undergo serious doubts as to who we are and why. It involves being open to alternative ways of framing the situation and this can come with a degree of 'deskilling' – we can feel lost and vulnerable without our 'old truths' to hold on to. In reflective practice, writes White et al. (2008: 10), the familiar theories and practices need somehow to be 'made strange'. It is also, of course, exciting, and comes with an invitation to communicate with practitioners 'outside our own milieu' as part of 'trying on' new perspectives (Etherington, 2004: 9).

ABOUT YOU, THE REFLECTIVE LEARNER

Reflective practice is going to be explored with reference to raw emotions as well as with cultural, political and epistemological aspects in mind. The chapters that follow will explore both your 'gut' reflections and your more philosophical emotions via ongoing references to case studies and practice. There will also be a number of reflection points and activities for you to work through. At this stage I would encourage you to obtain a notebook and call it your 'reflective practice manifesto'. This manifesto or 'dialectic notebook' (Carter and Gradin, 2001: 7) will form a record of your personal reflective practice 'journey' and is likely to involve several stages of writing and perhaps some painting or collage work as part of the process of absorbing and dealing with your impressions. To be 'messy' is part of the process of exploring life from new angles. We will examine the concept of a reflective practice manifesto in more depth in Chapter 2.

LEARNING HOOKS

You will be encouraged to examine your own reflections throughout the book. An important assumption in this book is that learning takes place through engagement. Frank Smith (1985: 172) lends us the metaphor of 'learning hooks' to capture how our attention and interest sometimes extend and cause us to engage. Comprehension requires engagement, asserts Smith:

> *The hooks that go out when engagement occurs are the hooks that are necessary for any understanding, for 'grasping' a situation or a story.*

Certain things in this book will capture your attention and connect with your learning hooks more than others. However, we hope that your thoughts around reflective practice will extend beyond the pages within. Your learning hooks will, hopefully, extend into your everyday life through actions, further reading and interactive moments.

Smith explores 'reflective writing' as a means of both understanding and creating 'reality'. The 'relative permanence' of writing allows us to capture and examine our own attempt to 'constantly construct a theory of what the world is like' (Smith, 1985: 8).

THE 'DIALECTIC NOTEBOOK'

Dialectic engagement involves moving back and forth between opposing and different points of views:

> *The dialectic notebook is a tool for rethinking and reformulating ideas. Simply divide your page into vertical halves. As you read, you will keep a list of important quotations, ideas, words, themes, etc, together with page numbers, on the left hand side of the page. At some later time, you'll revisit the notes you made on the left-hand side, using the right-hand side of the page to make further comments . . . the right hand side will always be reflective.*
>
> (Carter and Gradin, 2001: 7)

An example of a dialectic notebook is given in Figure 0.1.

WHAT YOU WILL FIND IN THIS BOOK

Chapter 1 addresses the question 'What is reflective practice?' Reflective practice is explored in terms of 'owning' one's questions and problems, and transforming valuable learning into practice. Donald Schön's theory on reflective practice is as a point of departure as we move into the subject of practitioners' analytical 'frames'. Recent developments within reflective practice (Fook, 2002; Bolton, 2005; Taylor, 2006) bring concepts such as subjectivity and reflexivity to the forefront. These will be introduced with an 'emancipatory' (Fook, 2002) interest in mind.

'Owning' one's questions involves being open to one's potential blind spots and biases, rather than shunning, disowning or displacing them. This involves abdicating from an expert stance to a reflective positioning where we consider our own contribution to a problem area. Our underlying personal, cultural and theoretical values and assumptions will be explored

Dialectic notebook with quote etc. on one side and own thoughts on the other, gathered during reading about reflective practice.

Snippets of information	My own thoughts
'Haiwaiian Psychology is the integration of the traditional Hawaiian culture with psychological theories, practices, beliefs and customs for healing' (Rezentes 2006: 132)	*Is there a typical Swedish version of therapy? Is there any underlying difference between Swedish, Spanish and English therapy?*
'Countertransference, then, has to do with the analyst's capacity to be wounded' (Sedgwick 2005:108)	*Compare with van Deurzen's thinking about ongoing personal therapy for the therapist.* ↓
'Unlike trditional shamans, modern-day healers are expected to be psychologically strong, robust, and stoical . . . As incongruous as it may seem, the profession that aims to assist people in accepting and coming to terms with their feelings and needs often fail to tolerate or even acknowledge such human concerns in its practitioners'	*How 'strong' shall a therapist be? Check up on Guggenbuhl-Craig and what he says about owning up to our vulnerabilities, rather than 'dumping' them on others.*
'Social work as a practice is facing transformation of the welfare state and its position is problematic' (Fook 1999:36)	*Guggenbuhl-Craig compares social work, nursing and teaching with psychotherapy. Check out more about where counselling and psychotherapy stand in today's society. Is therapy affected by 'the transformation of the welfare state'?* *. . . and check up what Fook actually means with transformation of welfare state . . .*

Figure 0.1: An example of a page from a dialectic notebook

with reference to us, the authors of this book, and with regard to yourself and your choice of career. Our practice will be explored from a cultural, epistemological and psychological angle with a combined interest in the practitioner's unique self and his or her 'culturally tinted lenses'. There can be no objective stance, argues Ian Parker (1994); even a stance of distance is a positioning. This is an assumption explored with reference to Schön and Argyris's concept of 'double-loop learning' and their distinction between espoused theory and theory-in-use.

In Chapter 2, counselling and psychotherapy will be explored in terms of 'listening with both hands' (Symington, 1986). It involves 'hearing' both the spoken and the unspoken messages in the room. A question that runs throughout the book is raised in this chapter: 'How can we as therapists hear the unspoken without putting our own words into the client's mouth?'

The chapter is concerned with the therapist's unique self. With reference to double-loop learning, you will be encouraged to consider what brought you into therapy in the first place. The idea of 'helping' others will be explored as a very powerful position with both dark and light sides to it. How may this affect your practice?

We will consider some of the pitfalls of the 'wounded healer'. As suggested earlier, Guggenbuhl-Craig (2009: 83) warns of the risk of 'projecting illness completely on to the patient and identifying himself exclusively with the healer pole'. Jungian therapists often stress the value of 'wounds'. As we shall see, Sedgwick (1994: 108) explores countertransference as something that 'inevitably residues with one's own wounds'. Countertransference is linked to the therapist's ability to be wounded, and Sedgwick proposes that projections will hook on to individual therapists for different, special reasons. Like Guggenbuhl-Craig, Sedgwick insists on the importance of 'getting to know your own shadow' in order not to enact it. You are expected to explore your own potential 'wounds'. This chapter resonates with the thinking addressed by Hawkins and Shohet (2008: 9), who write:

> *We believe that is essential for all those in the helping professions to honestly reflect on the complex mixture of motives that have led them to choose their current profession and role.*

In Chapter 3, our 'hearing' is further explored with reference to the idea of 'culturally tinted glasses'. Therapeutic practice will be viewed in the light of postmodern and post-structural thinking, with a focus on how language conveys and creates meanings at both an individual and a cultural level. 'Meanings' do not simply emerge from within individuals but develop in the context of specific interactive episodes. This chapter focuses on the impact of social and cultural values and beliefs on both the therapist and the client. Meaning-making processes are considered with reference to postmodern thinking about 'local' truths as opposed to the idea of universal truth, which has characterised the technological, progress-driven society that most of us know. The idea of 'local' truths is considered with reference to concepts such as narratives and discourses. Political conflicts are, according to many feminist writers, missed and ignored in the postmodern debate. Its deliberate stance in postmodernism against dogmas and truths can sometimes bring an idealised picture of modern society. There is, many groups argue, a hidden political aspect of locally held values; some voices are more easily heard than others. It is also what is *not* said that shapes our view of ourselves and others. Individual stories of identity are situated in cultural discourses about good and bad, right and wrong. Post-structuralist thinking, as expressed by Foucault, asserts in a similar way that there is an inherent power involved in our selective discourse about inclusions – for instance, in terms of sanity and normality.

You are encouraged to consider the underlying cultural, political and social assumptions that you may or may not bring with you into the room. The term 'critically reflecting practitioner' is a core concept in this chapter.

Basic beliefs and subsequent ideas about 'truth' and knowledge in therapy are explored further in Chapter 4. An underpinning principle in reflective practice is the need to be open to alternative ways of framing problems and situations. The concept of 'epistemology' is also introduced, with its focus on basic underpinning beliefs from which knowledge is generated and inferences are made in our daily work.

What is, first of all, counselling and psychotherapy? From what basic belief about reality and about our profession do we infer and generate further knowledge in therapy? The issues around how our basic underpinning beliefs impact on our different ideas about 'truth', and how to go about generating knowledge will be explored further with reference to epistemological theory. Schön's theory will be explored with reference to older philosophers such as Kant and Dilthey who, in the eighteenth century, addressed the difference between human studies and natural sciences. The neo-Kantian philosopher Dilthey distinguished between one mode of reflection aiming to 'understand' (*Verstehen*) and another aiming to 'explain' (*Erklärung*).

The *Verstehen*-based reflection approaches human beings as unique, interactive, interpreting individuals, and the *Erklärung*-based reflection focuses on humans as one of a kind, with explanations that derive from biological sciences. Dilthey argued that understanding was the only interpretive method appropriate for human studies. This assumption will be explored in the light of the ongoing debate around evidence-based practice. What can natural scientific explanations tell us about human beings? The debate often reinforces the antagonism between the two basic beliefs regarding different interpretive frameworks.

In spite of a seemingly clear-cut distinction between an expert and a reflective practitioner, Schön draws our attention to how reflective practice can involve a carefully considered balance between the two. A perspective combining an empathic, reflective understanding with professional expert stance is explored in the context of what the philosopher Ricoeur (1970: 187) refers to as a dialectic relationship between a 'narrative' and 'explanatory' commitment when interpreting clients in psychotherapy.

Different forms of understandings in therapeutic practice will be put into the context of today's emphasis on evidence-based practice. In Chapters 5 and 6, Dr Biljana van Rijn, Head of Clinical Practice at the Metanoia Institute, writes about how evidence-based and reflective practice may complement each other. She offers an overview of development in evidence-based thinking to assist you as a practitioner in navigating the requirements for evaluation and is well positioned to grasp concerns that practitioners experience in 'real life'. Schön stressed the importance of linking theory to practice; he wanted to avoid elaborating on fine theories that failed to work in the 'swampy lowlands of practice' (Schön, 1983, cited in Taylor, 2008: 78). An underlying theme in van Rijn's chapter is how to reconcile the requirements of evidence-based practice with the sensitivity and flexibility involved in both counselling and psychotherapy.

The debate around evidence-based practice often involves references to quantitative research as a means of 'evidencing'. The term 'researcher' is often used in a 'cold' neutral way; we picture a scientist in a laboratory cut off from the world outside. Quantitative methods are, however, not the only sources of evidence. Therapy can be seen as a collaborative process involving exploration, interpretation and ongoing joint 'testing'. Therapeutic practice is often underpinned by what, in research language, is often referred to as participatory action research methodology, allowing the participants to 'create their own knowledge and theory relevant to their own specific situations' (Ellis and Kiely, 2000). This book expands on what qualitative research can offer evidence-based practice. We have devoted a separate chapter to research. In Chapter 7, Professor Simon du Plock writes about work-based and reflective learning with the aim of 'demystifying' research. Professor du Plock elaborates on the theme of making tacit knowledge explicit through practice-based research. As the head of a practice-based doctorate programme for psychotherapists, Simon is also well equipped to talk about reflection in a practical, real-life context.

The idea behind having three authors of this book is based on the idea of 'critical friends'. Critical friends have little, if anything, to do with being 'critical'. The term refers to someone, such as a trustworthy friend or colleague, who understands where you come from and is able to throw new light on a situation and assist you with your 'blind spots'. Reflective practice is ultimately a social process; it involves feedback and the injection of new, sometimes foreign, angles from others. Simon, Biljana and I share an interest in reflective practice, but you will notice that we approach the subject from different angles. Biljana, for instance, is more experienced in evidence-based practice and will share her knowledge and practical experience from tutoring and supervising within this particular domain. Simon is experienced within work-based research and will share his particular expertise in a demystifying manner.

You will also note that we each have a different writing style. We have deliberately kept it this way, to illustrate the point that narratives both create and reflect different meaning, values and beliefs. You will be encouraged to consider the difference in our three different 'voices'. Does Simon, for instance, reflect your assumptions about researchers and academics? Does Biljana 'speak' like an 'evidence-based' clinician? What are your expectations of academics, practitioners etc. and why?

Chapter 8 involves tying all this together in a coherent framework. By this stage you will have encountered the concept of 'transformative learning' through real-life references in the Preface (Sofie's story) and through Simon's account of his systematic inquiry into chronic fatigue. In this chapter you are expected to complete your manifesto, with transformative learning as a final stage of your reflective practice cycle. Transformative learning involves an 'extended abstract' stance where a problem is being transferred, related and compared with principles and ideas in other areas. You are encouraged to identify a scenario that could prevent your practice from moving forward. This could be an existing problem or an issue that you believe may cause problems at a later stage. Perhaps you struggle with ending sessions, with fees or with keeping your time boundaries? Or maybe you find it difficult to say 'No' and are beginning to fear 'burnout'? Some of you may find yourself caught between conflicting underpinning values, like Allan and Liza who you will meet later on. Your own reflective writing will hopefully have brought some thoughts, themes and more explicit insights to the forefront regarding areas for personal improvement.

This chapter is based on two models. The first has already been introduced with reference to Atherton's 'taxonomy' or hierarchical classification, as developed by Moon (2004) and Roffey-Barentsen and Malthouse (2009). It relates to five levels of understanding involving noticing, making sense, making meaning, working with meaning and the eventual transformative learning. Each level builds on the knowledge and insight required at the preceding level. Incorporated in the stages is the SMART model, also borrowed from Roffey-Barentsen and Malthouse (2009) who address the model separately. SMART stands for Specific, Measurable, Achievable, Relevant and Time-bound.

You will be encouraged to make an assessment of your own needs and subsequent actions. This book aims to prepare you to engage with your supervisor around your needs as a practitioner. We suggest that you consider your needs for best practice on three levels:

- your personal needs for support, for instance, personal therapy and peer groups;
- your educational needs in terms of further reading, workshops, training and continuing professional development;

- the implications of ethical and professional requirements, which will prompt you to reconsider professional boundaries, such as confidentiality, on an ongoing basis. What do you need to do to meet these requirements?

ACTIVITY 0.1

In her theory about supervision Proctor (1986) refers to ethical, educational and personal needs in terms of 'normative', 'formative' and 'restorative' needs. Consider the following questions and make a list of at least five examples for each.

- Your normative needs: in what ways can you assess and consider your practice with regard to professional and ethical guidelines, norms and laws?
- Your formative needs: in what ways can you receive feedback or direction in order to develop skills, theoretical knowledge and personal attributes as a practitioner?
- Your restorative needs: how are you listened to, supported, confronted and challenged with regard to your personal issues, doubts and insecurities?

CHAPTER 1

What is reflective practice?

CORE KNOWLEDGE

This chapter introduces the idea of 'owning' our questions in a way that challenges the idea of a completely objective stance within the helping professions. The following key terms will be explored:

- *reflection* and *reflective practice*;
- *reflection in* and *reflection on practice*, as distinguished between by Donald Schön, e.g. thinking on your feet versus looking back at your work afterwards;
- *double-loop learning*, a concept introduced by Schön and his colleague Argyris to explain how underlying values and assumptions affect our strategies and decision making at work;
- the concepts of *espoused theory* and *theory in use* introduced y Schön and Argyris to explore the interesting gap between what professionals say they do and how they actually practise;
- Donald Schön's definition of *framing*, also looking at recent developments within reflective practice (Fook, 2002, Bolton, 2005; Taylor, 2006) where concepts such as *subjectivity*, *reflexivity* and *critical reflection* are explored with an 'emancipatory' (Fook, 2002) interest in mind;
- *reflective writing* – explored as a form of reflective practice that involves taking advantage of the 'relative permanence' in our written work that means we can return to, linger over and reconsider our own meaning making processes.

REFLECTIVE PRACTICE IS ABOUT HARNESSING TRANSFORMATIVE LEARNING

Reflective practice prompts questions about *what* we know and *why*, i.e. how we come to know it. Being reflective involves the practice of examining our own meaning making processes. It is a process that can be traced back to the work of Socrates with the idea of learning through questioning and feedback.

Carter and Gradin (2001: 2/5) expand on the concept of reflection and encourage us to look at things in the *light of ourselves*. How do we throw light on the problem at hand? What do we focus on and what is ignored?

> *Notice the metaphor in the word, reflection. Think of the subject of your reflection as the reflective surface . . . and yourself . . . as the light source. When you examine the subject in your own light, what do you see? . . . Look at what you know and think and begin to ask questions. How did I know that? Why do I think this? Was it something I experienced? Did I learn this from a book?*

WHY SHOULD WE KNOW ABOUT THIS?

What is the value of knowing all this? Well, as we shall see, reflective practice has much in common with the underpinning principle in counselling and psychotherapy about transforming negative experiences into valuable wisdom and knowledge. It is the alternative to ignoring or escaping a problem, or displacing it. Inspired by the thinking of John Dewey that learning inevitably builds on mistakes, problems and errors are viewed in context of their possibilities: if you can't beat them, join them, so to speak. Learn to *know* the problems and *utilise* them!

What is reflection? The process of reflection involves, as White et al. (2008: 41) put it, 'examining our experiences and assessing what is reflected back'. They emphasise how this questioning often involves new and different meanings. Reflective practice is about 'harnessing this learning':

> *This may also involve constructing a new meaning, or one which makes sense in a new or different circumstance. What is important, of course, is that if we are to harness this learning, we become much more aware of the process and the new meanings we are making. This is in essence the basic idea behind reflective practice.*

DIALECTICAL ENGAGEMENT

Reflective practice involves more than just looking at ourselves in a mirror; it involves a form of 'dialectical engagement':

> *By dialectical, I mean an engagement that is ongoing and recursive [meaning roughly repeated, looping back on itself] as opposed to a single, monetary encounter. In the process of trying to understand an*

> *other, our own beliefs and assumptions are disclosed, and these assumptions, themselves, can become objects of examination and critique.*
>
> (Carter and Gradin, 2001: 4)

Bolton (2005) emphasises that reflective practice is, as Bolton (2005) emphasises, not about 'navel gazing' but about 'dialectical engagement' (Carter and Gradin 2001), which involves the ability to move between oppositional images. It involves considering yourself and your culture through the lens of another culture. The ability to 'try on' new perspectives and world views and critically reassess ourselves, our ideas, our values and assumptions is often referred to in terms of 'reflexive awareness'.

Transformative learning involves an ability to take a broad view of a problem. If we need to fix a small problem with a car, for example, it is necessary to understand how cars work generally. 'Making sense' is the stage referred to here; after noticing a problem, we can either focus on escaping it or roll up our sleeves with a view to identifying the exact nature of the problem. 'Making meaning' is the next step in the repair process. Some problems can be fixed temporarily with sticky putty! Reflective practice involves more durable solutions and exploring the different parts of a problem in the context of the whole with the goal of finding out 'what goes where'. 'Working with meaning' takes place when connections between separate parts of the whole are being made. A recurring problem with clients overstaying or 'forgetting' to pay can, for instance, be considered in the light of your own personal assumptions about your work; maybe you feel deskilled and inadequate – not worth the money? If so, where does this come from? Reflective practice involves looking at the client's behaviour in the light of you – and what will be referred to in this book as your shadow. To transfer new insights into practice is the final step. The road to this point usually requires considerable planning, which is what the action plan in Chapter 8 is designed to assist you with.

KEY THINKERS

Socrates (469–399 BC)

Socrates is referred to as one of the founders of Western philosophy. He has lent his name to the concept of 'Socratic method' in which people with opposing viewpoints engage in a 'dialectical' argument. One hallmark of Socratic questioning is that there is more than one 'correct' answer. Socratic dialectic arguments encourage us to think more about exactly what we are saying with our arguments. Basic 'tell me more' questions – Why are you saying that? What exactly does this mean? Are you saying x or y? – urge us to go deeper in ways that are familiar to most therapists.

The probing of assumptions also provokes us to consider unquestioned beliefs on which we found our arguments: You seem to be assuming . . . ? How did you choose those assumptions? What else could we assume? How can you verify or disprove that assumption? What would happen if . . . ?

Socratic reasoning makes us think twice about what we call 'evidence'. When describing our 'evidence' behind the arguments the difference between fact and fiction often opens up, through questions such as: Why is that happen-ing? How do you know this? Show me . . . ? Can you give me an example of that? What is the nature of this? Why is this happening?

John Dewey (1859–1952)

Dewey is often referred to as the forerunner of progressive education – in particular, the student-centred schooling that gained influence during the 1960s. He coined the phrases 'learning by doing' and 'critical thinking'. No knowledge claim, argued Dewey, is ever certain or immune from criticism and revision. Knowledge is a 'living' thing, always developing and depending on new perspectives. The idea of students as 'empty vessels' is, subsequently, an inappropriate way of approaching education. There is no absolute knowledge; knowledge develops all the time through interaction between people and their environment. Education must respond by being flexible and by provoking intelligent, experimental inquiry.

Dewey distinguished between 'routine action' (Paige-Smith, 2008) and 'reflective action'. In routine action, we respond to external circumstances through habits and traditions without active consideration. This requires passive learners like empty vessels. In contrast, reflective action requires carefully considered and justified responses to situations.

Donald Schön is often regarded as the 'father of reflective practice'. He coined the phrase in 1983 with his book *The Reflective Practitioner*. Although this chapter will explore reflective practice with particular reference to Donald Schön's original theories, we will also look at how reflective practice has been linked to concepts such as reflexivity and critical reflection.

KEY THINKER

Donald Alan Schön (1930–1997)

Donald Schön researched and wrote for over 40 years about organisational learning. He was often associated with Harvard scholar Chris Argyris, and both were influential thinkers in developing the theory and practice of reflective professional learning in the twentieth century. Schön's book *The Reflective Practitioner* (1983) challenged practitioners to reconsider the role of technical and instrumental knowledge in favour of more open, social and reflective inquiry. This thinking gained huge influence in teacher education, health professions and architectural design.

Frame Reflection is another well-known title by Schön, published in 1994 and co-authored with Martin Rein. Schön's theory on 'framing' challenged the way politicians and policy makers based 'framings' of social problems. Schön argued that policy making often rested on tacit, 'taken for granted' knowledge, rather than seriously considered and reflected-upon information.

Schön invited managers and decision makers to move beyond a purely rational model of understanding to a more inquiring, social and reflective approach to problems.

REFLECTION-ON AND REFLECTION-IN-ACTION

Schön distinguishes between reflection-on and reflection-in-action. Reflecting-on is something that we do when looking back on our work: what did I do right and where did I go wrong? Schön uses the concept reflection-in-action for reflections that takes place while doing, i.e. when in action. He compares reflective practice to artistry, where the practitioner combines already acquired skills with the ability to be totally open to new perspectives. Like the artist, the reflective practitioner is aware of the many faces of 'reality'. Depending on light and shading, positioning and angles – and, of course, technique – the artist is able to capture the world in sometimes very different ways. Much of this happens while thinking on one's feet. This is a familiar process to those engaged in therapeutic practice.

Most counsellors and psychotherapists commit themselves to the value of frame reflection without actually being aware of it. Every time that you tell your client that they may not be able to change the event itself but that they can alter the meaning(s) that they attach to it, you adhere to the value of frame reflection. You imply that by reframing our understanding of life, real changes will follow.

Schön (1983: 130) observes that there are 'many competing views' within therapy:

> *There is controversy not only about the best way of solving specific problems, but also what problems are worth solving, and what role the practitioner should play in their solution.*

REFRAMING PROBLEMS

In all types of therapy, observes Schön, finding the problem is a problem in itself – the therapist 'must construct an understanding of the situation as he finds it' and he 'approaches the practice problem as a unique case'. Schön describes this as 'the conditions for reflection-in-action' (Schön, 1983: 129).

REFLECTION POINT

Most counsellors and psychotherapists approach each client account as a unique combination of events and experiences. The counsellor's assessment of 'lack of trust', for instance, differs from the medical doctor's diagnosis of a 'case of' mumps or measles. Mrs Jones's lack of trust may share certain conditions with Mrs Brown's acquired lack of trust; but they are not the same symptom requiring identical treatment. In fact, argues Schön, it is the therapist's job to explore the unique meaning and to understand the very specific combination of experiences and events.

In doing this, not only the client's but also the therapist's pre-understanding needs to be taken into account. Tacit, implicit assumptions will need to be made explicit.

Consider what impact a strongly held religion can have on work with issues such as abortion or divorce, when approaching each client problem as unique.

Psychotherapy, reasons Schön, rests on reframing and reshaping situations. Whether the therapist adheres to a modality that conceptualises the clients' framings in terms of an 'organismic valuing process' (Rogers, 1961) or as 'object-splitting and internalisation' (Fairbairn, 1952), constructing new understandings of a situation is what therapy is all about – it is a generic trait of the trade, and Schön (1983: 130) writes:

> *I propose that by attending to the practitioner's reflection-in-action . . . it is possible to discover a fundamental structure of professional inquiry, which underlies the many varieties of design or therapy advocated by the contending schools of practice.*

In other words, Schön suggests reflection-in-action as a path to an integrated perspective on counsellors' and psychotherapists' work. He thinks that there is an underlying structure for professional enquiry that transcends therapeutic 'varieties' or modalities – something that different therapists have in common.

INFORMED PRACTICE

Action strategies within mental health, social care and education are difficult to measure. Schön's theory on reflective practice explores two different ways of monitoring quality. We can, on the one hand, look at the 'problem' with a set understanding of cause and effect in mind. Freud's drive theory lends us an example of a predetermined understanding about the human mind. Sexual drives as a primary motivational energy of human life guided Freud's hearing of women whom he diagnosed as suffering from hysteria, for instance.

KEY THINKER

Sigmund Freud (1856–1939)

Freud is a thinker who has shaped twentieth-century psychology, but as Holmes and Bateman Holmes (2002: 4) point out, 'Freud was first propelled towards the invention of his "new science" for quite mundane and practical reasons.'

Although Freud was a prominent neurologist in the 1880s, his career opportunities were limited by the already thriving anti-Semitism of the time. Married and with a growing family, Freud decided to build up a private practice around hysterical symptoms, which, he had witnessed, 'thronged the physician's consulting rooms' at the time. Freud was inspired by Charot and Janet, the latter of whom postulated a seemingly successful hypnotic treatment of hysterical phenomena. Together with his colleague Breuer, Freud found that by putting clients into a hypnotic trance and asking them to speak freely about their troubles, symptoms appeared temporarily relieved. In collaboration, Breuer and Freud documented their progress in *Studies in Hysteria*. Holmes and Bateman write:

> *Their 'cathartic' approach centred on the idea that neuroses resulted from the 'damming up' of painful affect, and that, like the lancing of a boil, if mental distress could be released via its verbal expression under hypnosis, relief would follow.*
>
> (Holmes and Bateman, 2002: 4)

Freud abandoned hypnosis and further developed the method of free association, at first with a focus on actual early trauma, which led to the belief that hysteria was the result of unconscious conflicts concerning sexuality. He pictured the inner world as wish-based and pleasure principle-driven in nature. Freud used the term 'resistance' when clients showed signs of experiencing conflicting drives. The aim of analysis became to 'work through' this conflict so that memories and drives could surface to a conscious level, rather than being 'acted out'. As Symington (1986) suggests in his book *The Analytic Experience*, Freud developed his ideas continuously. His thinking needs to be understood in the context of the time and culture within which he worked. Even today, the mind is treated as an alien feature compared to the tangible nature of limbs, bones and organs.

Of particular importance for reflective practice is Freud's work *The Interpretations of Dreams*, in which he explores the meaning of 'repression' (1938/1959: 51) with reference to his own reactions towards his parents and extended family. Many agree that it is in his work with dreams that Freud really began to develop a theory about the mind.

One event in particular that influenced psychoanalysis as we know it today was the occasion when a client flung her arms around Freud's colleague Breuer. Freud began to explore the idea of 'transference', which he later (1938/1959: 38) referred to as follows:

> [T]he patient sees in his analyst the return – the reincarnation – of some important figure out of his childhood or past, and consequently transfers to him feelings and reactions that undoubtedly apply to this model . . . This transference is ambivalent: it comprises positive and affectionate as well as negative and hostile attitudes towards the analyst, who, as a rule, is put in the place of one or other of the patient's parents, his father or his mother.

To explore transference as a re-enactment of the patient's core difficulties subsequently became one of the defining features of modern psychoanalysis.

Freud's famous case study from *Fragment of an Analysis of a Case of Hysteria* can, with hindsight, be compared to what Schön and Argyris refer to as 'single-loop' learning. Freud rationalises his client Dora's repulsions of her father's friend's approaches as a symptom of 'repressed' sexuality and Oedipal wishful fantasies. What later on angered feminist writers, in particular, was how Freud linked Dora's problem to her own suppressed sexuality without putting his cause-and-effect thinking of women with 'hysteria' in a social, cultural context. Nor did he challenge his own motives in 'pathologising' Dora for expressing repulsion to attention offered by the family friend whom Freud describes as 'perfectly desirable, albeit a little older, man'.

REFLECTION POINT

Bolton emphasises the responsibility of the practitioner to consider values and beliefs. Reflective practice 'is not a mere quietist navel-gazing', writes Bolton (2005: 5), and he continues:

> *Reflective practice work can become politically, socially and psychologically useful . . . It supports, demands even, practitioners' thinking about values . . . Values which underpins practice are rarely analysed and questioned.*

Consider the idea proposed by feminist thinkers that symptoms such as hysteria and anorexia are 'problems of society carried by the individuals'. What is a 'socially constructed' problem?

Freud's drive theory is not only critiqued by feminist writers as suppressive in its own right. Others have referred to it as 'quaint and naïve' (Sussman, 1992). Indeed, Freud himself developed his ideas radically over time. He continued, however, to hold on to the idea of the analyst as the 'clean surgeon' – an idealised picture according to many of his followers. Winnicott is an example of a clinician who owned up to strong feelings such as hate. In his article about hate in countertransference (1938/1959), he emphasises the importance for 'the analyst's own hate [to become] extremely well sorted-out and conscious'.

We will return to the Jungian view on countertransference, in particular, with its emphasis on the therapist's own wounds and 'hooks' for the client's projections to latch on to.

Simply put, countertransference is concerned with the therapist's personality structure. Holmes and Lindley (1998: 126) write:

> *Transference refers to the ways in which the feelings, wishes and actions of the patient in relation to the therapist may be unconsciously influenced, coloured and distorted by earlier childhood experiences. Countertransference, on the other hand, comprises both the therapist's 'blind-spots' – her unconscious and childhood-derived wishes and fantasies in relation to the patient – and affective responses of which she is aware, which can be put to good use in helping her to understand the patient.*

In his study about unconscious motivations for practising psychotherapy, Sussman concludes that the view of therapists has undergone irrevocable change since the concept of countertransference was introduced. Sussman (1992: 259) writes:

> *[T]he clinical and conceptual simplicity of the one-person model of psychotherapy has long since vanished . . . Those of us who practice psychotherapy can no longer afford not to explore our own motivations to heal.*

Research summary

Reflection involves 'examining our experiences and assessing what is reflected back'; this often involves self-reflection. 'Know thyself before you set out to act in the world', writes Carter and Gradin (2001).

Reflective practice is, as White et al. (2008: 41) put it, about 'harnessing this learning' and becoming 'more aware of the process and the new meanings we are making'. Reflective practice raises an awareness of how our own, often hidden, assumptions and theories are translated into practice. Fook (2002: 38) writes:

> *The reflective approach recognises that theory is often implicit in the way professionals act and may or may not be congruent with the theory they believe themselves to be acting upon.*

Reflexivity, asserts Fook, 'takes this further, drawing attention to the perspective of the knower' and encourages us to explore other perspectives. Reflexivity requires us to 'try on the perspective, the world view of an "other" for long enough to look back critically at ourselves, our ideas, our assumptions, our values' (Carter and Gradin (2001: 4). Fook brings the concept of reflexivity to the forefront in reflective practice. Reflexivity encourages us to 'try on' other perspectives and regularly reconsider the impact of our own theoretical, personal and cultural, political underlying values and beliefs:

> *What we see and understand in a situation is influenced by our 'subjectivity' including our embodiment (e.g. race, gender, social position, sexual orientation ability, age) biography, values, ethics, emotions, cognitive and theoretical constructions.*

In social sciences, cause and effect is difficult to think of in terms that Guggenbuhl-Craig (1991) refers to the 'two-plus-two-makes four' principle, which single-loop learning is ultimately about. Argyris and Schön (1978: 2–3) distinguish between single-loop and double-loop learning:

> *Single-loop learning is like a thermostat that learns when it is too hot or too cold and turns the heat on or off. The thermostat can perform this task because it can receive information (the temperature of the room) and take corrective action.*
>
> *Double-loop learning occurs when the error is detected and corrected in ways that involve the modification of an organisation's underlying norms, policies and objectives.*

A single loop is 'completed within a single coherent frame of references' (Hawkins and Shohet, 2008: 79). It concerns explicit, expressed and often officially adhered to objectives and strategies (Figure 1.1).

Hawkins and Shohet (2008: 78) illustrate double-loop learning (Figure 1.2) with reference to seemingly unproblematic situations that, when delved into, involve hidden agendas:

> *[The second learning loop] explores attitude, values and assumptions. This second loop ensures that the learning is deepened beyond the most obvious. It is the second loop that actually digs below our questions and finds new ones. For instance, a supervisee might learn within a single loop that clients may be erratic in their attendance if a clear contract is not made, but when the learning has a double loop they may understand, for example, why they are drawn not to make a clear contract with the client who shares with them the difficulty in accepting authority.*

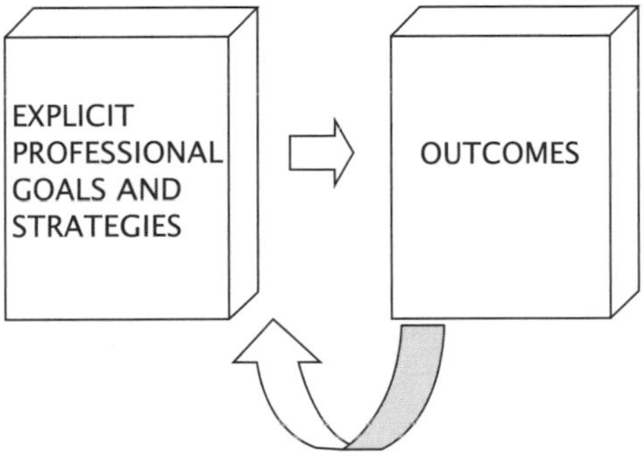

Figure 1.1: Single-loop learning

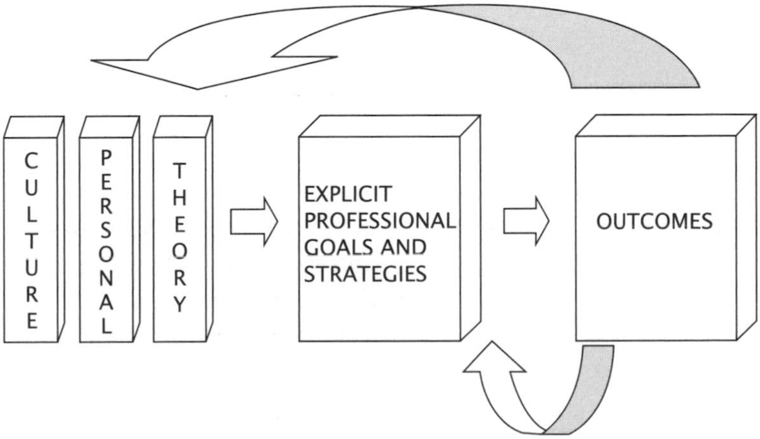

Figure 1.2: Double-loop learning

Double-loop learning helps to expand our analytical frame 'beyond the obvious' (Taylor, 2006), to explicitly identify and challenge underlying cultural, personal and theoretical assumptions. It invites the practitioner to consider their own underlying assumptions behind their expressed goals and strategies.

Double-loop learning requires a different way of looking at objectivity. Parker (1994) asserts that we must abandon the positivist definition of objectivity. Even when we think that we are being neutral and detached by keeping a distance between ourselves and our 'objects' for work with either clients or research, we are inevitably producing a subjective account; a position of distance is, stresses Parker, still a position.

An example of double-loop thinking for Freud would have been to challenge his own underlying assumptions regarding men and women. In this sense, double-loop thinking turns the problem back to the assessor or the so-called 'knower' and encourages questions such as 'How do I "know"?' or 'What underlying personal, cultural and theoretical assumptions may influence my understanding of the "problem"?'

EMANCIPATORY KNOWLEDGE

Strategies in both work and life in general are often based on a complicated pattern of beliefs and values that can be held as facts until unveiled and challenged. Double-loop learning builds on the idea of expanding the analytical and emotional framework. Sometimes it involves freeing oneself from others' values and beliefs, which we may previously have regarded as 'facts' about something. These can be both personal and culturally imposed values, as addressed earlier with reference to the implication of early psychoanalytic references to women and hysteria.

FAILING TO PRACTISE WHAT WE PREACH

Schön and Argyris apply the term 'espoused theory' to what people say and consider themselves as adhering to at work. Our espoused theory is what we officially commit ourselves to. However, in one of their surveys, Schön and Argyris found that, in reality, people often failed to implement their espoused theory. People did not do what they said or even thought they would do. The professionals, in other words, did not practise what they preached. Argyris and Schön (1978: 6–7) found a discrepancy between practitioner-espoused theory and their 'theory-in-use'. An important point with this research was that the absence of the espoused theory more often than not surprised the practitioners themselves. This obviously caused complications when strategies failed to work; people looked for problems in the wrong places:

> *When someone is asked how he would behave under certain circumstances, the answer he usually gives is his espoused theory of action for that situation. This is the theory of action to which he gives allegiance, and which, upon request, he communicates to others. However, the theory that actually governs his actions is his theory-in-use [with implicit values and assumptions, often taken for granted].*
>
> (Argyris and Schön, 1978: 6–7)

The reasons for this gap are many, ranging from unconscious decisions to organisational, cultural factors obscuring the practitioner's own insight. In the following case study, Allan explores his couple counselling work in supervision. Allow yourself time to consider Allan's underlying assumptions and how, if at all, his espoused theory matches up with his theory-in-use.

Case study 1.1 Allan

Allan has worked as a relationships counsellor for seven months. He is training to be a psychodynamic counsellor and has chosen the psychodynamic path because of how the theory resonates with him. The way our past seeps into our present makes a lot of sense to him. He enjoys couple work and is particularly interested in work with unconscious motivations and how they affect the way we choose our partner. Allan has tried to introduce the idea of unconscious fit in different ways; he wants to capture the essence of psychodynamic thinking but he is not quite sure how to do this. He uses a map and a diagram, which makes it quite clear. He thinks of it as throwing light on to people's shaded areas. Allan has, however, been unable to engage with any more long-term work. While many of his peers have developed a portfolio of cases, Allan is still predominantly involved in assessments; his longest case so far is four sessions. He senses resentment and resistance in most couples, and feels that people are afraid to commit. Allan explores another 'non-starter' with his supervisor. Below is a section from the supervision.

'So, they never gave any explanation to why they didn't come back?' asks Pete, the supervisor.

'Well, I had a feeling that they mightn't come back,' says Allan. 'I had a hunch.'

'Tell me . . .'

'I felt that the wife wasn't all that serious, she seemed to be going along . . . you know, pretending to be serious . . .'

'Serious about what?'

'You know, serious about staying . . .about working on it, repairing the relationship.'

'What was their presented problem again, remind me . . .'

'The couple met in 2007, had a baby almost immediately.'

Allan looks at his papers.

'Trouble communicating . . .,' he reads. 'They didn't talk, never had, according to the wife.' Allan closes his file and adds:

'I gave them homework, we met three times, and not once had they done their homework.'

'What kind of homework?'

Allan shifts uneasily in his chair.

'You don't sound too pleased . . .,' he says.

'You mentioned that the wife wasn't serious . . . serious about what, I wonder?'

'About staying!'

'Why should staying in the relationship be an obvious goal to your work?'

'Well, if I only can help one couple to stay together, if I save one set of lives, I'd be happy. You don't know what it's like to separate.'

'It seems like none of your clients return for more than a couple of times at the most. I am wondering if you work with an agenda that's your own rather than focusing on the clients.'

'What's my job about if not keeping people together?' exclaims Allan.

'I would argue that your job is to provide space and opportunity for people to explore their situation in as undisrupted a way as possible. How do you see it?'

'Well, isn't that what I'm doing? Aren't we talking about exactly the same thing – about helping people with their lives?' asks Allan with a frustrated look.

REFLECTION POINT

- How could Allan's goal of helping people stay together be construed differently? Compare Allan's views with those of his supervisor, Pete. Allan thinks that they are talking about the same goals. What do you think?
- What underlying assumptions may affect the way Allan construes his role? What may affect his outlook on work?
- To what extent does Allan implement his espoused theory, the psychodynamic theory? How would you describe Allan's theory-in-use?
- What are Allan's personal and theoretical underlying assumptions? Do his espoused theory and theory-in-use match up?

YOUR REFLECTIVE PRACTICE MANIFESTO

It may seem ironic that a book revolving around a practice geared towards listening should begin with an emphasis on writing. We will explore different approaches to your own thought processes and their implicit and explicit effects on your practice, but writing is proposed as an ongoing important theme to consider.

The relative permanence of writing

The importance paid to writing is based primarily on what Smith (1985: 33) refers to as 'the relative permanence' of writing. Unlike speech, writing has the benefit of allowing us to return to, linger over and reflect upon what we have constructed in our own mind:

> *Writing is an extremely efficient way of gaining access to knowledge that we cannot explore directly. It is more efficient that speaking in many respects because of its relative permanence and because we can stand back and examine it as an independent entity.*
>
> (Smith, 1985: 33)

Your manifesto is a 'composition' (1985: 33) in the sense that Smith uses the term; your piece of writing is a reflection of your brain's natural activity. Your composition, your own writing, involves several layers of processing and will, at the same time, offer a 'space' to recognise and identify these processes – the result of your own imagination. We are, asserts Smith, not normally aware of our creative nature of the brain:

> *We are certainly not usually aware of constructing hypothetical worlds as we go about the daily commerce of our existence . . . we can [usually] only be aware of our imaginings as they are manifested.*
>
> (Smith, 1985: 33)

For a reflective practitioner, gaining a better understanding of the way we organise events and experiences into what we eventually come out with as 'true' or 'valid knowledge' is an intrinsic capability.

Smith stresses the value of writing as a means of accessing our 'theory' about reality:

> *We cannot observe ourselves thinking, but we can observe the products of thought. And one of the most powerful tools for doing so is writing.*
>
> (Smith, 1985: 33)

Bolton, too, emphasises the importance of writing. She quotes Pattison, and writes:

If we had asked people to talk about their values in abstract terms, we would have received responses. By asking them to tell [write] stories about important experiences we were able to see something of how values reveal themselves in a complex, varied and shifting way in practice.

(Bolton, 2005: 9)

In their book about writing as a reflective action, Carter and Gradin (2001: 6) conclude that 'reflective writing' helps us to 'make explicit what we think about things'. As suggested initially, reflection is about challenging our own conclusions. Writing helps us to look at what we know and think, and begin to ask the important questions: How did I know that? Why do I think this? Was it something I experienced? Did I learn this from a book?

Smith proposes that we demystify writing. He suggests that it is 'unproductive' (1985: 16) to regard writing as an activity that requires esoteric skills, unusual talents or lengthy training. Writing is rather 'an extension and reflection of all our efforts to develop and express ourselves in the world around us'. Writing both reflects and creates meaning; it 'helps us to make sense of [the] world and to impose order upon it'.

The product of your thoughts

A composition, proposes Smith, usually involves three different stages and moves from fleeting thoughts and impulsive reactions to a more structured version of events that can eventually be reflected upon and explored with regard to themes and patterns, for instance.

The stages in your reflective writing can be compared with the existentialist philosopher Jean Paul Sartre's idea of a 'multi layered nature consciousness'. Finlay and Gough (2003: 111) write:

Reflection . . . aims to effect a more direct contact with experience as lived . . . To better understand the connection between reflection and reflexivity, we can turn to the work of Sartre . . . [he] distinguishes between

1) Unreflective consciousness . . . where the self is an active agent – taken up by living in the moment . . .

2) Reflective consciousness – here the self and experience become [our] object of reflection

3) Self-reflective consciousness . . . [where] the self becomes the object of reflection . . . re-focus on ignored aspects . . . self-reflect on prejudices . . .

We suggest that your composition, i.e. your manifesto, involves four stages, which are described below. You are encouraged to compose your manifesto around the question 'What do I need to be a reflective enough practitioner?' Note that the fourth stage revolves around talking about, discussing or sharing your manifesto with your supervisor – aim to arrive at the final stage with your own needs and interests clearly in mind.

Stage 1: Prewriting, or 'incubation' stage

This is a busy phase in your learning when you approach reflective practice from all angles. The incubation stage, argues Smith (1985: 122–25) is usually a 'frustrating' time:

> *Incubation is mysterious because it is difficult to specify what exactly the brain is doing except in such general and non explanatory terms as exploring, hypothesizing, testing and integrating.*

This is a stage where you gather information from all around you, experientially from role plays, own practice, training events, and so on. You will hopefully bring an interest in reflective practice into both your personal and professional life. Allow yourself to be inspired and engaged. And be prepared to scribble and be 'messy'. Maybe you will choose to draw or paint – or perhaps use other materials or media to channel and capture impressions and reactions. Reserve this stage of the writing as a 'note-keeping' stage. Your dialectic notebook is likely to be scribbled in considerably during this stage. Smith writes:

> *An important part of prewriting is the making of notes, whether in carefully kept diaries and notebooks or in jotting on scraps of paper like old envelopes; [w]hat I should call disposable writing.*
>
> (Smith, 1985: 126)

In Smith's opinion, prewriting is a particularly valuable and interesting time for us if we wish to bring our unconscious processes into awareness. Your prewriting section will be an important stage in your work. You will probably revisit this and pick and choose from your notes, for a more 'reflexive' account of your reflective practice.

Stage 2: Actual writing

If the prewriting stage is a note-keeping phase, the writing stage could be seen as a diary-keeping phase. This is a stage when thoughts are surfacing and where spontaneous reactions and observation can be captured in a diary, for instance. Allow thoughts to 'pour out' – a sense of 'order' or structure may start to emerge.

There is still something immediate about this stage; you can be impulsive at times, and the text can revolve around emotions and observations that you may not necessarily want to share with others. You will probably return to your scribbles with an interest in linking it all together in order to best capture who you are and what you have to deal with at work.

Stage 3: Rewriting

This is your own response or, as Smith (1985: 127) puts it, a stage where 'the writer responds to the text as if it was written by someone else'.

It is a little like finding an old diary in the attic and then approaching documented teenage infatuations looking for patterns and themes: Why did I change partners so often? Was that way of dealing with things typical of me? How have I changed? What are the recurring themes in my life? In other words, what do you think of your first draft of your reflective practice manifesto? Does it reflect what you actually want to say and what you actually think or agree with? Does the manifesto capture your needs in relation to personal issues, learning and ethical concerns?

Stage 4: Talking, sharing

This stage revolves around communication. Your communication with a supervisor about your underlying assumptions and potential blind spots in practice is an essential part of this process. Consider themes and patterns when you explore your work with cultural, personal and theoretical influences in mind. This book will prepare you for that. Presentation-wise, you may choose to work with bullet points and lists.

So write with your supervisor in mind. Tease out themes; if you have many long lists, try to pick out main areas of interest to explore further with your supervisor. If it helps, arrange your text around Figure 1.2, the double-loop learning figure on page 23.

Expand your analytic frame to identify and challenge underlying cultural, personal and theoretical assumptions that may impact on your practice.

The key to success

'Good enough'

Your manifesto should revolve around your needs in order for you to be a 'good enough' practitioner. Hawkins and Shohet (2008: 3) write about the 'nursing triad' that Winnicott stressed as important in order that parents can be 'good enough':

> *The late Donald Winnicott, paediatrician and psychoanalyst . . . points out that it is very hard for any mother to be 'good enough' unless she herself is also held and supported . . . This provides the 'nursing triad' . . . The concept provides a very useful analogy for supervision, where the 'good enough' counsellors, psychotherapist or other helping professional survive the negative attacks of the client through the strength of being held [themselves].*

- What do you need in order to feel supported in being a 'good enough' practitioner?

Thoughts and processes

For your manifesto you will need to be prepared to:

- scribble and make notes in the margins of the other books that you read and/or in your dialectic notebook as soon as anything resonates with or concerns you;
- make notes, sometimes 'disposable ones', about aspects that latch on to your 'learning hooks';
- take yourself seriously and consider your thoughts and feelings as important. Set aside time to 'listen to yourself' (Smith 1985: 125) – this 'requires a certain quietness so that we can literally hear and reflect upon the ideas that come to us';
- be creative, playful and tolerant to false starts and wrong turnings; your mind is already guided by your imagination and the creativity to deal with unknown, new events in your daily life. These exercises revolve around tuning into already ongoing processes and bringing them into awareness. Depending on your previous experiences of education, you may need to leave some of your old views on learning behind;
- have confidence in yourself, trust your writings and rewritings. There are no rights or wrongs. Your manifesto is there to assist you, and your clients – not to please any teachers or book editors!

Uninterrupted writing

There is often a fear about not being 'able' to write, as if there is a set way of writing. The point of reflective writing is to make maps of your own learning. It is not about being shortlisted for the Booker Prize!

An essential step is to get going. To do so, we recommend some 'uninterrupted writing': write for ten minutes without stopping. As Winter et al. (1999: 11) advise:

> *Uninterrupted writing [means] to get down and write. If you cannot think of the next word, then repeat the one you are writing until the one you need occurs to you. Don't spend time wondering what to write next.*

ACTIVITY 1.1

- Continue writing from the sentence below, for ten minutes without stopping!

  I remember it was a school day, maybe a Tuesday or a Wednesday. I was sitting on my bed, looking for a sock, thinking that . . .

When you have finished, return to your text.

- What does it feel like to write about yourself?
- To what extent does writing about yourself reveal, conceal or maybe misrepresent? Was there anything that you chose to avoid? Or perhaps something that words failed to express?
- Can you see any links between the school day in your text with how you feel here and now, at the beginning of this book?

CHAPTER SUMMARY

You have been introduced to the following stages of reflective learning: noticing, making sense, making meaning and transformative learning. The final stage involves the ability to position an initially isolated problem in a larger context through systematic inquiries.

Schön insisted that managers and decision makers should move beyond a purely rational model of understanding to a more inquiring, social and reflective approach to problems. Schön encouraged us to approach recurring problems in our practice with the following question in mind: is there a mismatch or a contradiction between:

- our 'espoused' theory of action = the values we say we are going to enact? and
- our 'theory-in-use' = what we actually do? Schön found that the theory-in-use often conveyed tacit, implicitly held norms and assumptions about the world, applied without a real awareness of their impact.

Schön and Argyris coined the concept 'double-loop learning' to capture the idea that learning helps to expand our analytical frame 'beyond the obvious' (Taylor, 2006), to explicitly identify and challenge underlying cultural, personal and theoretical assumptions.

- Single-loop learning is 'completed within a single coherent frame of references'.
- The second learning loop explores attitudes, values and assumptions and ensures that the learning is deepened beyond the most obvious. Double-loop learning invites the practitioner to consider their own implicit, underlying assumptions behind their expressed goals and strategies (see Figure 1.2 on page 23).
- In this book, reflective practice and reflexivity are treated as overlapping and complementary concepts, as Fiona Gardner (2008: 145) proposes:

  [Reflective practice] is an approach in which the learner is encouraged to be as reflexively aware as possible of their social, political and psychological position, and to question it, as well as their environment.

Kondrat distinguishes between three 'alternative perspectives on practice' (ME Kondrat, cited in Gardner, 2008).

- *Reflective self-awareness* involves the capacity to be aware of our own biases and preferences – for instance, through the choice of theory and way of relating to our clients. A guiding question here is to what extent we are congruent with our 'espoused theories'. Do we practise what we preach? If not, why not?
- *Reflexive self-awareness* involves considering what impact our own personal history and culture have on the way we interact with others. How do your own experiences and environment affect your choice of modality and the way that you choose to approach therapeutic practice?
- *Critical reflexivity* concerns the link between us and our social structure. Bolton (in Gardner, 2008) emphasises that 'we all wear culturally tinted lenses through which we view the world.' This encourages us to think about how gender, race, religion and social expectations might have shaped our attitudes towards ourselves and other people.

SUGGESTED FURTHER READING

Bolton, G (2005) *Reflective practice – writing and professional development.* London: Sage.

This book is filled with exercises and will give you a good sense of both reflective practice and reflective writing.

Finlay, L and Gough, B (2003) *Reflexivity: a practical guide for researchers in health and social science.* London: Blackwell.

Do not be put off by the word 'researcher' in the title. This is a selection of comprehensive texts that make the topic reflexivity less 'scary'.

Reidmond, B (2006) *Reflection in action: developing reflective practice in health and social service.* Aldershot: Ashgate Publishing House.

The book offers a very good general overview of reflective practice. It tells you everything you need to know about the origins of reflective practice and how it has developed over time.

White, S, Fook, J and Gardner, F (2008) *Critical reflection in health and social care.* Maidenhead: Open University Press.

This book expands on the topic 'critical reflection' through accessible texts from several different writers. It is particularly recommended for those who are interested in exploring the links between social values and assumptions and the way we frame our world views. It will give you an excellent insight into how gender, religion and culture can affect practice.

CHAPTER 2

Personal values and assumptions

The 'wounded healer'

CORE KNOWLEDGE

- This chapter examines the personal underlying values and assumptions that a counsellor and psychotherapist may bring into the room. This means that we will focus on our personal material in the double-loop learning model.
- The term 'listening with both hands' (Casement, 2008a) is explored here with reference to how we may relate to and 'hear' both the spoken and the unspoken messages in the room. How do we, as therapists, hear unspoken messages without putting words into the client's mouth?
- The idea of 'helping' others will be explored as a very powerful position with both dark and light sides to it. With reference to double-loop learning, you will be encouraged to consider what brought you into therapy in the first place.
- The concept of 'wounded healer' will be explored. The 'rescuing trap' will be examined in terms of Guggenbuhl-Craig's (2009: 83) warning about 'projecting illness completely on to the patient and identifying himself exclusively with the healer pole'.
- Jungian therapists often stress the value of 'wounds'. Countertransference is being linked to the therapist's ability to be wounded, and Sedgwick (1994: 108) explores countertransference as something that 'inevitably residues with one's own wounds'.

EMOTIONAL REFLECTIONS

Throughout this chapter, you are encouraged to reflect upon your own *emotions* as part of your framing. This puts 'reflexive self-awareness' into the forefront.

You will be encouraged to consider: What is going on inside you when you listen to others? What do you feel before thinking?

Hate and love are introduced as two strong feelings inevitably stirred in therapeutic practice. How can such strong emotions be used as assets rather than as a hindrance to your practice? And what are the options for counsellors and psychotherapists to have emotional responses independently observed and verified, in accordance with evidence-based practice?

The double-loop learning model may assist you to structure and make your own framing-process more accessible.

HEARING 'DEEPLY'

'When I can really hear some one,' writes Carl Rogers, 'it enriches my life.' Hearing 'deeply' means to 'hear the words, the thoughts, the feeling tones, the personal meaning, even the meaning that is below the conscious intent of the speaker' (Rogers, 1995: 8). Rogers describes hearing as one of life's 'sparkling moments', where individuals connect with something universal:

> *There is [a] peculiar satisfaction in really hearing someone: It is like listening to the music of the spheres, because in the immediate message of the person, no matter what that might be, there is the universal. Hidden in all the personal communications which I really hear there seem to be orderly psychological laws, aspects of the same order we find in the universe as a whole. So there is the satisfaction of hearing this person and also the satisfaction of feeling one's self in touch with what is universally true.*
>
> (Rogers, 1995: 8)

Rogers describes hearing as a truly beautiful thing, 'like the music of the spheres'. For many therapists, negative feelings towards clients can be uncomfortable to consider or discuss. However, the Jungian analyst Paola Valerio stresses that love and hate are inseparable aspects of a relationship – a fusion of opposites:

> *I . . . work with patients where strong countertransference feelings ranging from irritation to actual repulsion and hatred of patients, were judiciously disclosed and worked with in the consulting room. Hate is more commonly written about in relation to work with severely disturbed or borderline patients, but in my experience it is a more frequent occurrence that is usually acknowledged in work with all patients, if the analyst is open to it.*
>
> (Valerio and Mann, 2002: 264)

Valerio emphasises an important point often made in psychoanalytic literature: namely, that negative *and* positive feelings are there. The question is not whether or not they exist, but whether the therapist 'is open to it'. This does not make 'hearing' any less valuable and it does not make the therapist a less honourable person. Hate and love are strong feelings that are invariably stirred in emotionally intense processes, and they can be a great asset to the work when properly considered:

> *When love and hate are treated as mutually excusive the tendency is to idealise the one and demonise the other. [But] as Winnicott noted (rather radically for his time), the mother hates her infants from the word go, for all sorts of good reasons. Primitive feelings of love and hate are inevitably stirred up in this analytic vessel.*
>
> (Valerio and Mann, 2002: 264)

This chapter will focus on hearing outwardly as much as inwardly, with a focus on how your own reactions can be used as assets rather than obstacles. The starting point for this discovery is *you*. You will be encouraged to concentrate on your own reactions. Your own emotional, intellectual and social material will be regarded as crucial contributions to the 'story' told by your client.

KEY THINKER

Carl Rogers (1902–1987)

Rogers is the one of the most influential psychologists in American history. He is the founder of humanistic psychology, and he established the person-centred approach to understanding personality and human relationships, which has found wide application in various domains such as psychotherapy and counselling. Towards the end of his life he was nominated for the Nobel Prize for his contribution to peace and conflict resolution. Apart from counselling and psychotherapy, Rogers has contributed significantly to the field of education. He has authored 16 books, some of the best known of which are: *Client centred therapy* (1951), *On becoming a person* (1961), *Freedom to learn* (1969) and *A way of being* (1980).

ACTIVITY 2.1

You need a partner for this exercise, which focuses on *listening*. You will each take turns to talk about a personal subject for five minutes without any interruptions at all.

Go through this checklist before you start:

- Have you got a watch?
- Is the speaker comfortable?
- Have you explained to your partner that this exercise is for you to explore your role as listener?
- Have you agreed on what to do if any unforeseen strong emotions should arise?
- Is the speaker prepared to talk without interruption for five minutes? Five minutes can feel like a long time.

Consider the following:

- What did it feel like to talk without any intervention?
- What happened during your five minutes of listening?
- What did you feel inside while the other person was talking? Anger, sympathy, boredom, distraction, inadequacy, involvement, excitement? Aim to be as honest as possible with yourself; the replies need not be shared. Concentrate on connecting with *all* strong emotions during listening – what happens inside you when listening?
- How did the other speaker feel after completing this activity? Discuss how it felt to talk for five minutes.

THERAPY AS ARTISTRY

We referred earlier to the idea of 'listening with both hands'. To recap, this involves listening to the client's verbal messages while at the same time paying careful attention to the unspoken messages in the room – with regard to both the clients' signals and our own.

REFLECTION POINT

Schön (1983: 130) compares the multifaceted skills of a therapist with that of an artist:

> *[The psychotherapist] gives an artistic performance . . . in his selective management of large amounts of information, his ability to spin out long lines of invention and inference, and his capacity to hold several ways of looking at things at once without disrupting the flow of inquiry.*

Is this an image that you can relate to?

To embrace reflective skills akin to those of the artist involves an openness to the suggestion that life can look different depending on where you try to 'capture' it. However, even if you are artistic and bring materials into the room with which to work creatively, the ultimate work should not rely upon sharpened pencils but on you – you bring only yourself as a tool, as Guggenbuhl-Craig (2009: 73) points out:

> *We work with our own psyche, our own person, without instruments, methods of technology. Our tools are ourselves, our honesty, our own personal contact with the unconscious and the irrational . . .*

Sedgwick (1994), Sussman (1992) and Guggenbuhl-Craig (2009) are examples of analysts and researchers who argue that therapy can reach only as far as the therapist himself has been able to reach. Strupp (in Sussman, 1992: 6) found in his research that the 'therapist's personal influence outweighs the effects of particular techniques on treatment outcome.'

As suggested earlier, with reference to the concept of a 'good enough' practitioner, all counsellors and psychotherapists require plenty of support to 'bring the best' out of themselves. The following section will focus on what you may need for your own well-being, in order to provide the best possible service for your client.

MIRRORING SINGLE- AND DOUBLE-LOOP LEARNING

Supervision is a kind of 'mirroring' (Knott and Scragg, 2008: 23). The mirror reflects back to us 'what is going on' and 'helps us to recognise what we are feeling as well as thinking'. We need feedback to help our learning both during and after work.

Ironically, receiving help is often a mixed blessing for a 'helper'. It is a seldom talked about subject, but many counsellors and psychotherapists struggle with the fact that they 'need' to undertake personal therapy as part of their training. The majority will quickly realise the importance of therapy, but some remain unconvinced, at times nurturing a sense that therapy is for others.

Sussman (1992: 246) identifies an intolerance within our profession with regard to our own weaknesses:

> *Unlike traditional shamans, modern day healers are expected to be psychologically strong, robust and stoical . . . those who become openly depressed or anxious are liable to be viewed by colleagues as somehow inferior or weak . . . As incongruous as it may seem, the professional that aims to assist people in accepting and coming to terms with their*

feelings and needs often fails to tolerate or to even acknowledge such human concerns in its practitioners.

ACTIVITY 2.2

Take some time to consider the purpose of counselling and psychotherapy.

Using the following text as a starting point, write for ten minutes without interruption.

> Claire had considered therapy for some time, yet she felt surprised when she finally heard a voice at the other end of the phone. Claire cleared her throat and said 'I'm looking for a therapist who might help me with . . .'

What reasons did Claire have for seeking therapy? On what did you base your writing? Was it your own or others' experiences?

Most counselling and psychotherapy training requires that trainees undertake personal therapy. As we shall see later, replies to a recent survey (Bager-Charleson, 2010) about why people choose to become a therapist indicate that one's own personal therapy can throw a new light on an individual's motives for becoming a counsellor or a psychotherapist in the first place. This kind of 'mirroring' can be painful – our whole sense of self sometimes needs to be re-evaluated. Reflective practice exposes aspects of ourselves that we have perhaps learnt to avoid. In their book about supervision in helping professions, Hawkins and Shohet (2008: 9) write:

> *We believe that it is essential for all those in the helping professions to honestly reflect on the complex mixture of motives that have led them to choose their current profession and role.*

COUNTERTRANSFERENCE AND PROJECTIVE IDENTIFICATION

Another important usage of the term *mirroring* in psychotherapy is in the context of the actual therapeutic relationship. Some psychodynamic terms for this kind of mirroring are *transference*, *countertransference* and *projections*. In their book about reflective practice in social work, Knott and Scragg (2008: 73) refer to transference and countertransference in a slightly wider sense than we did in the earlier references to Freud. They write:

> *[C]ommunication may be at a non-verbal level. For example, a person who uses services who was depressed spoke to me in a calm, quiet*

> *manner, but I felt uncomfortable, I was becoming tense. I realised that I was mirroring his tension, which was incongruent with his speech. Transference, i.e. of his tension, and countertransference, i.e. my becoming tense, are psychoanalytical concepts which can help to understand your interactions.*

This form of mirroring or feedback can be difficult to trace, but to do so could be argued as crucial. The understanding of this intricate combination of spoken and unspoken messages in the room is framed differently, depending on modality. *Projective identification* is a term used in psychodynamic theory for the mixed feelings that can arise when two people are relating to each other. In Knott and Scragg's example above, the narrator becomes the recipient for the other person's disowned feelings. Cashdan (1988: 56) writes:

> *[With projective identification] it is as if one individual forces another to play a role in the enactment of that person's internal drama – one involving early object relationships.*

Projective identification usually happens without people being aware of it; neither the 'projector' nor the recipient may be conscious of anything other than the feeling, the mere sensation:

> *The recipient is 'pressurised' to think, feel and behave in a manner congruent with the ejected feelings and self- and object-representation embodied in the projective fantasy.*
>
> (Cashdan, 1988: 56)

The term 'pressurised' refers to processes that take place outside both parties' awareness. The actual projection usually stems from an underlying, denied fear of a particular outcome. Take the following example:

> Max always came across as agreeable. He never raised his voice but had a habit of being late and forgetting to keep promises. Sandra, his wife, would nag and argue; Max had thought she seemed different from his extremely strict mother but was beginning to 'see' the resemblance, which confirmed his belief that no woman would ever stand by him and like him for who he was.

In this example, we can see that Max is 'projecting' his strong feelings on to his wife and is in the process of recreating his blueprint 'horror' scenario as a result. Pushed to the limit, the wife reacts with anger and resentment 'just like his mother'. Cashdan (1988: 65) concludes:

> *The husband's projective identification acts as a way of both discharging a projective fantasy [about relationships and self] and of manipulating his wife to respond in a circumscribed way.*

The term 'projective identification' captures an important phenomenon in therapy where the therapist can use his own reactions to understand something that 'belongs' to the client. Cashdan (1988: 139) goes as far as suggesting that whatever feelings are stirred in the therapist can be understood in the light of the *client*'s pathology. He writes:

> *The therapist functions as an internal counterforce that enables the patient to combat – and ultimately let go of – the destructive object relations that existed beforehand.*

This implies – and it is not so different from what Freud indicated towards the end of his career – that the therapist should, and actually could, be construed as 'fully analysed' – as sterile as a surgeon. Whatever the therapist feels can be regarded as 'information as a means of identifying the patient's pathology' (Cashdan, 1988: 101).

MIRRORING FOR THE 'WRONG' REASONS

Others emphasise the importance of therapists challenging their own infallibility. When exploring how to 'listen with both hands', Casement encourages a more self-critical approach. He emphasises the importance of 'mirroring' as a kind of 'trial identification with the patient, listening to oneself from the patient's point of view'.

Casement (2008b: 148) explores an example in which the therapist has been late for an appointment, and then the client has missed their subsequent appointment:

> *[T]his is what I mean by criticism by mirroring. The patient unconsciously enacts a version of the therapist's failure. It is now she who gets the time wrong, but it could be a way of holding up a mirror to him, about the previous day.*

Jung (in Sedgwick, 1994: 15) emphasises that the therapist must 'at all times keep watch over himself' and ask 'what does this patient mean to me?'

Jung also writes about a 'hook' for the projections to latch on to – a subject to which we will return:

> *Experience shows that the carrier of the projection is not just any object but is always one that proves adequate to the nature of the content projected – that is to say, it must offer the content a 'hook' to hang on.*
>
> (Jung, cited in Sedgwick, 1994: 108)

Jung and many other Jungian analysts stress the danger of not knowing about and admitting to our 'shadow'. Guggenbuhl-Craig (2009: 73) writes:

> *People are most cruel when they can use cruelty to enforce the 'good'. 'We must refrain from playing the part of someone who never falls into the shadow and must be prepared to admit our mistakes with this regard.*

The concept of 'shadow' refers here to the shadow archetype that Jung reserved for the 'aspect of the self that seeks to disavow and project outside itself'. Most therapists undergo personal therapy that, together with ongoing supervision, eventually become essential 'audit points' for making the therapist's 'knowing in action' explicit. Guggenbuhl (1991: 113) continues:

> *The future analyst becomes conscious of his shadow during the course of a good training and control analysis.*

KEY THINKER

Carl Jung (1875–1961)

In 1908, when the first psychoanalytic congress took place, Freud admitted Jung as the first non-Jewish disciple and 'ring bearer'. Freud had special rings made for progressive physicians and intellectuals with an interest in developing the psychoanalytic movement. Jung was initially viewed as Freud's 'crown prince'. He could not, however, reconcile himself with the way Freud insisted on the centrality of sex and his suspicion of religion, and in 1910 Jung left Freud and became the founder of analytical psychology.

Guggenbuhl-Craig warns that knowing one's shadow is never a completed project; it is a matter of ongoing reflection. The unconscious is, as Jung points out, 'necessarily out of our awareness'. Guggenbuhl-Craig continues:

> *[H]ere we come up against the tragedy inherent in being an analyst. The greater and broader the analyst's growing consciousness becomes, the greater in turn grows his unconsciousness. Unconsciousness, and along with it the problem of falling into the shadow, is the great problem of the analyst . . . An honest analyst will realise with horror from time to time that in his daily work he has been acting exactly like an unconscious quack and false prophet.*
>
> (Guggenbuhl-Craig, 2009: 37)

In his book *A Curious Calling* Sussman explores conscious and unconscious motivations for practising psychotherapy. He proposes that many psychotherapists risk using their clients as the 'mirroring or idealised self objects' that they lacked as children. Sussman (1992: 102–03) writes:

> *The role of psychotherapist can place an individual in a unique position to receive admiration and idealisation from others . . . The power differential that is inherent in the therapeutic relationship can contribute to the therapist's sense of superiority . . . [M]ost therapy clients are plagued with self-doubt and low self-esteem, predisposing them to take a subservient position . . . That allows for and fosters the therapist's narcissism and need to be iconised.*

At the beginning of this book, we referred to Alice Miller's suspicion of 'wounded healers', and many therapists have themselves experienced neglect or abuse as children. In a survey about why therapists choose to become therapists (Bager-Charleson, 2010), 280 counsellors and psychotherapists were approached with the following questionnaire:

Why choose to be a therapist?

Which of the following resonates most with you?

1. I have always been *interested in people*.
2. I enjoy *the analytical, investigative element* of therapy most.
3. The *flexible working hours* were essential when considering a career.
4. I believe that my *own childhood* influenced my choice of career.
5. A *crisis in later life* brought me into therapy and raised my interest in working as a therapist myself.
6. None of the above resonates with me; instead I chose to work as a therapist because of . . .

The majority of the 280 therapists said they had chosen to become therapists because of childhood (4) and adult events (5). Many referred to a combination of childhood events that left them ill-equipped to deal with a subsequent adult event such as bereavement or divorce. For many, the crisis became a turning point in life. Several therapists recognised that they had embarked on therapy training as a roundabout way of dealing with their own problems. One of the respondents, Lisa, illustrated how some therapists recognise this through their own subsequent training. Lisa began her training guided by motives that only later became clear to her. What Lisa felt originally was an interest in people but with a focus on vigilance rather than on sensitivity, something that today she connects with her own abusive childhood.

ACTIVITY 2.3

How would you respond to the survey?

- Insert the following heading in your manifesto: 'Why I chose to be a therapist'.
- Choose one or more motives from the list in the survey above.
- Expand on your motives using a maximum of one page. If it helps, write as you speak, as if you were being interviewed.

The idea of a 'wounded healer' is regarded as an asset by some, such as Sedgwick and Jung. Others, such as Miller and Sussman, are more critical, as we addressed earlier. Most therapists agree, however, that when dealt with reflectively, the therapist's own 'baggage' can become a valuable tool. Van Deurzen asserts that a therapist is always challenged and thus never 'fully analysed':

> *There is to my mind no such thing as being fully analysed or being able to take a neutral stand . . . As therapists and counsellors we are constantly tested and altered by life, just as much as our clients are . . . we make our living through employing our own personality, our character, our life experience and ourselves in relations. As such we put ourselves inevitably at risk.*
>
> (van Deurzen, 2009: 106)

ACTIVITY 2.4

The rescuing trap

Hawkins and Shohet (2008: 9) warn against the omnipotent helper who harbours 'omnipotent fantasies of changing others or the world, when we cannot change ourselves'. Being a 'good enough' therapist requires, as suggested earlier, that we look after ourselves.

The British Association for Counselling and Psychotherapy (BACP) ethical guidelines below are usually considered carefully by counsellors and psychotherapists with regard to their clients and their needs. But good practice actually requires that therapists also apply the guidelines to themselves. Do you do that?

Transfer the ethical guidelines below into your manifesto. To what extent do you meet the guidelines?

Fidelity Am I being true to myself? Do I really want to see this client? Is it right for me, my family and friends, to take on this client at this stage? Do I need more time for myself?
Autonomy Am I considering all factors in my own life when I take on this case? Am I making an informed decision with regard to my own needs and interests right now? Do I 'know' what I am doing, right now, with my own needs in mind?
Beneficence Where are my own interests in all this? Is this choice serving my own best interests? Am I considering both the short- and long-term effects on myself – for instance, psychical and emotional effects?
Non-maleficence Am I possibly doing myself harm with my decision to take on a new client, to work evenings or to continue working in general?
Justice What price might I be paying to help others? Am I doing myself justice? Am I fair to myself? If not, why? And what do I need to find a comfortable balance?

After this exercise, take some time to return to the here and now. Allow yourself to leave your own practice behind, and immerse yourself in the case study below when you feel ready.

The case study illustrates the complexity involved in listening inwards and outwardly at the same time as considering theoretical and practical frameworks.

A reflective therapist needs to ask him or herself:

- What is the client communicating verbally and non-verbally?
- What am I 'hearing' and how?
- What do I feel?
- What do I think? How do I structure and frame the information that I receive? Where does my understanding of the present situation come from? Could I frame my understanding in any other way?

Read the case study with these questions in mind, and reflect on how Sarah appears to be handling the concerns.

Case study 2.1 Sarah and Pat in supervision

Sarah is a psychodynamic psychotherapist with a placement in an agency where she receives fortnightly supervision. She also practises from home. Sarah usually strikes her supervisor as an enthusiastic and inquisitive person, and it is unusual for her to feel detached from work. But Sarah struggles with a new client, Pat, who is a night-time nurse with depression as her presented problem. Sarah normally writes two sets of notes; she presents brief comments for the agency and brings verbatim transcripts into supervision where she tries to recall her sessions word by word.

This is the second time that Sarah has reported feeling distant from Pat, and she struggles with remembering enough from the session even to write notes.

'I think I just *want* to forget the session,' admits Sarah. 'All I can remember is how time passes really slowly; I keep looking at the watch.'

After their last session, Sarah dreamt about Pat.

'I was desperate to find somewhere to sit . . . Pat expected therapy, and, well, it was embarrassing, stressful . . . it felt all wrong. Wherever we went there were kids and dogs and stuff,' says Sarah. 'Even my mum was there; she just walked straight in and started to talk about something to do with the house.'

Sarah looks annoyed and distant, and the supervisor wonders if she is enacting some of the experiences in the supervision. She looks for any message, verbal or enacted, for an understanding of Sarah's experiences with Pat. Sarah seems to be lost in thought and only eventually does she resume. She says that her feelings of not 'finding a good enough space' for Pat lingered long after the dream.

'I don't even really want to talk about her now either,' observes Sarah. She admits to feeling confused; she feels detached but at the same time the work with Pat feels almost intrusive or 'too close for comfort'.

'I'd like to map out to myself what's happening . . . like this,' she says and reaches for some paper. She divides the paper into a dialectical note.

'This is what she says, Pat . . . and this is what I see,' explains Sarah as she notes both *what* and *how* things had been said in their last session. Pat had kept her coat on, yet said, 'I really trust you.'

'And this is your voice,' she adds to her supervisor, '. . . when you talked about depression as anger – you know, when I felt so sorry for her that time. Well, I've been trying to use that, but it actually just made me even more confused. You said something about not feeling sorry for her . . . or not treating her like a victim, here!'

Distinguishing between what is actually said and what is done in terms of, for instance, body language, helps Sarah to explore her ambivalence. Pat's mixed messages become clearer. Sarah also realises how intrusive the supervisor's comment about 'depression as anger' has felt. The room seems crowded with voices and messages. The overriding theme, concludes Sarah, is her own issues around 'helping a helper', as she puts it to her supervisor. She is now able to explore how her own ambivalence has played into Pat's sense of unease and lack of trust. For both, the 'default position' is not to trust. Sarah has spent many years in personal therapy, but trust is an issue that returns in many disguises. Her supervisor secures space and feedback for Sarah to explore how best to deal with the issue this time around.

COUNTERTRANSFERENCE

Reacting to one's own reactions is an important part of daily work for a counsellor and psychotherapist. It involves several levels of reflection. The focus in this chapter revolves around our personal underlying values and beliefs. Countertransference is an example of how the therapist can relate to their own reactions in a relatively systematic way.

There are two extremes of looking at countertransference responses: one that assumes that the therapist's reaction has to be 'owned' by the client and his projections and one that assumes that the therapist's own 'pathology' is an important part of the equation.

Cashdan (1988: 101–02) highlights the first option when he depicts countertransference as ultimately a reaction to the 'patient's pathology':

> *Using the countertransference means reacting to one's reactions. This means allowing oneself to emotionally respond to the meta-communications embedded in the projective identification and using this information as a means of identifying the patient's pathology.*

However, as addressed earlier, Jung observed that for projections to really latch on there needs to be a hook. A projection will hook on to a therapist for a special reason. 'The carrier of projections is not just any object,' wrote Jung, 'but someone who offers a "hook" to hang on.'

This stance proposes that countertransference 'inevitably residues with one's own wounds' (Sedgwick, 1994: 108). Countertransference, suggests Sedgwick, is linked to the therapist's ability to be wounded. The charlatan or the quack falls into their shadow of omnipotence, believing themselves to be divine and ultimately relying on the patient to carry all pathology. The quack is unable to live his own life; he needs clients to live it for him:

> *The analyst caught in the shadow . . . stops living his own life altogether. . . The patients live, love and suffer for him.*

This brings us back to the 'rescuing trap' where the rescuers are 'using the patient to bear the burden of all the severe psychopathologies in the whole relationship' (Searles, in Sedgwick, 1994: 112). Hawkins and Shohet (2008: 9) assert that the more counsellors and psychotherapists are aware of their own shadow, the less need there will be for the therapist to make others carry what they cannot accept within themselves:

> *Focusing on our own shadow, we will be less prone to omnipotent fantasies of changing others or the world, when we cannot change ourselves. . .The 'crazy' psychiatric patient will not have to carry our own craziness, which we pretend to be completely sane . . .*

A COMPROMISE ON COUNTERTRANSFERENCE

Racker (2001) is a prominent voice in the area of transference and countertransference. He addresses how therapy involves a fusion between the past and the present for both therapists and clients. Countertransference 'embraces this complexity':

> *It is . . . this fusion of present and past, the continuous and intimate connection of reality and fantasy, of external and internal, conscious and unconscious, that demands a concept [e.g. countertransference] embracing the totality of the analyst's psychological response.*
>
> (Racker, 2001: 133)

Racker distinguishes between various types of countertransference, for instance *concordant* and *complementary* countertransference.

Clarkson (2002: 9) points at an important distinction between 'reactive' and 'proactive' countertransference. She reserves the first category for responses originating in the client:

- *Reactive countertransference* describes the psychotherapist's feelings that are elicited by or induced . . . by the patient.
- *Proactive countertransference* refers to feelings, atmospheres, projections etc. that can be said to have been introduced by the psychotherapist themselves.

REFLECTION POINT

Countertransference is a response to the need for therapists to react and reflect on their own reactions. Can you think of other ways, perhaps from other modalities?

ACTIVITY 2.5

Take some time to consider Sarah's response to Pat's behaviour.

- What impact, would you say, have Sarah's 'wounds' and her own trust issues had on her work with Pat? Where do Sarah's strong reactions fit in the countertransference debate? Is the reaction a projection from the client – a sign of the 'client's pathology' – or is it Sarah's 'stuff'? Or is it, perhaps, a bit of both?
- Try to recall something in your client work that has tapped into your own issues.

HEARING 'REFLECTIVELY'

Sarah's subsequent session brings drastic changes to the work. She begins to frame her understanding in terms of countertransference; she explores new sides to countertransference through discussions and reading. She considers Racker's and Clarkson's distinctions, and she experiments with thinking about her reactions in terms of a concordant, proactive type of countertransference. She explores the possibility that the atmosphere in the room may be instigated by her own rather than by Pat's emotions.

On an emotional level, Sarah gives herself space to mourn once again over what she never had herself as a child; she makes sure that she gets the support that she needs.

Facing her own shadow is a first step for Sarah to move out from an enacted and unconscious level. The next step is to explore the sensation, through feedback by a critical friend and through systematic inquiry – for instance, reading or further training. When she can put her initial reaction in a context, she feels able to focus on offering Pat space to explore the specific, unique meaning that Pat herself attaches to trust and mistrust.

THE REFLECTIVE CONTRACT

The idea of a 'sterile' therapist is not an unusual image in therapy or, indeed, in any other strand of the helping professions. The focus on reflective practice would be, for this kind of professional, on learning to 'read' the client's signal. Anger, resentment, fear, failure – all these would be important to identify and deal with. But ultimately they would be regarded as the client's belongings. This book takes a different stance and encourages the practitioner to engage with their clients in a 'reflective contract', as Schön calls it (see Table 2.1).

THE ALCHEMIC BATH

Schön refers to reflective practice in terms of a reciprocal process, where the practitioner's own uncertainty and openness are important components in the work. The reflective practitioner balances uncertainty with the curiosity of a child, exploring situations as if for the fist time with the determination of a scientist who refutes his hypothesis on the basis that it 'didn't work' and then tries again based on reflection-on-action. This gives reflective practice dialectical and reciprocal qualities, and both parties move between different, sometimes oppositional stances in order to find a truly new way of looking at things. Sometimes the psychotherapeutic process is referred to in terms of the 'third I'. Between the client and the therapist a 'third I'

Expert	Reflective practitioner
I am presumed to know, and must claim to do so, regardless of my own uncertainty.	I am presumed to know, but I am not the only one in the situation to have relevant and important knowledge. My uncertainties may be a source of learning for me and for them.
Keep my distance from the client, and hold on to the expert's role. Give the client a sense of my expertise, but convey a feeling of warmth and sympathy as a 'sweetener'.	Seek out connections to the client's thoughts and feelings. Allow his respect for my knowledge to emerge from his discovery of it in the situation.
Look for deference and status in the client's response to my professional persona.	Look for the sense of freedom and of real connection to the client, as a consequence of no longer needing to maintain a professional façade.
Source: Schön (1983:300).	

Table 2.1: Schön's reflective contract

springs out of the interpretation process when two individuals meet over a story. Buber (1947/1971) refers to the synthesis that emerges from the dialectic encounter between two separate beings and their stories, in terms of the 'realm of between': '(W)here I and Thou meet, there is a realm of "between"' (Buber, 1947/1971: 246).

Sedgwick contends that this meeting in 'the between' necessarily involves a 'mutual transformation'. Something happens when two people meet on this level, with an interest in bringing only themselves into the equation. Both parties are involved in a joint creation akin to what happens when two chemical mixtures result in a new, third component. Jung used the metaphor of an 'alchemic bath' to describe the 'gold' that can be created when new meanings are discovered, or rather 'created', in the therapy. Sedgwick (1994: 13) writes:

> *[T]he analyst and patient [are] both deeply involved in a psychological laboratory trying to create the 'gold'. As they experiment with and observe the elements, so to speak, it becomes evident that they themselves are intermingling. Each has his or her respective conscious and unconscious parts, which in turn pull on each other . . . Both parties are in a sense submerged in the potent, alchemic bath.*

In the case of Sarah and Pat, the meeting between the two people becomes, in this sense, a meeting of two frameworks. Hearing Pat's stories results in changes within Sarah; she is moved – disrupted even – and eventually enriched and ready for taking on board Pat's specific understanding of trust and mistrust, leaving her own shadow aside. She is ready to travel on Pat's side of the track so to speak; her own 'horizon', i.e. what she can see, is illuminated by Pat's understanding and outlook and vice versa.

ACTIVITY 2.6

Return to your manifesto. Insert the following heading: 'Dealing with my own strong reactions in the session'.

Search in your theory books, linked to your own modality, for at least three quotes with the following questions in mind:

- How does your modality guide and inform you with regard to strong emotions within the therapist?
- If you do not adhere to countertransference in the way Sarah does, how do you usually approach the issue of your own strong emotions that are raised while hearing?
- List the quotes on the left-hand side of the page and leave space on the right-hand side for personal comments, either now or later on.

CHAPTER SUMMARY

- This chapter revolves around the importance of 'getting to know your own shadow' in order not to enact it with your clients. You have been encouraged to explore your own 'wounds' and consider how these may affect your practice.
- The term 'rescuing trap' has been explored with reference to the potential need of 'helpers' for others to carry their vulnerabilities.
- Countertransference has been explored as a means for therapists to monitor and deal with their own strong reactions.
- You are encouraged to identify and consider what your specific modality offers with regard to dealing with the therapist's own emotions. How does it differ or coincide with the underpinning beliefs in the psychoanalytically inspired countertransference?
- The term 'reflective contract' is used with reference to a relationship between the professional and the client that is 'open for mutual learning'.

SUGGESTED FURTHER READING

Casement, P (1991) *Learning from the patient*. New York: Guilford Press.

Patrick Casement has authored a series of books about learning from patients. He encourages us to 'read people rather than spending too much time looking for answers in books'. Casement shares experiences through vivid case studies where mistakes, both one's own and others', are dealt with extensively. It is a good book for the student therapist about to enter into practice, particularly for those with an interest in psychodynamic thinking. But the book usually appeals to therapists regardless of therapeutic orientation.

Robbins, A (2000) *Between therapists: the process of transference/countertransference*. London: Jessica Kingsley.

Robbins's book about countertransference is an accessible text with role plays, image trips, fantasies and other group exercises. The book offers experiential insights into countertransference and invites the practitioner to 'open up new avenues' to client work.

Rogers, C (1995) *A way of being*. New York: Houghton Mifflin.

Rogers' texts are always filled with warmth, insight and reflection. This book gives a good overview of his own journey and development as a therapist. It also explains the key concepts, processes and philosophy behind person-centred therapy.

Yalom, I (1991) *Love's executioner: and other tales of psychotherapy*. London and New York: Penguin Books.

Love's executioner is a classic among readers wanting to find out more about therapeutic practice. Although the book falls under the category of existential therapy, most readers agree that the book covers universal problems in therapy. Yalom's introduction gives a flavour of the poetic and at the same time insightful tone that runs throughout the book:

> *I do not like to work with patients who are in love. Perhaps because of envy – I, too, crave enchantment. Perhaps it is because love and psychotherapy are fundamentally incompatible. The good therapist fights darkness and seeks illumination, while romantic love is sustained by mystery and crumbles upon inspection. I hate to be love's executioner.*

CHAPTER 3

Culturally tinted lenses

CORE KNOWLEDGE

In this chapter, therapeutic practice will be viewed in the light of postmodern and post-structural thinking, with an interest in how language conveys and creates meanings on both an individual and a cultural level.

- Therapeutic practice will be explored with reference to the idea of 'culturally tinted glasses'. What impact might social and cultural values and beliefs have on therapists and their clients?
- 'Meanings', as Crossley (2000: 59) puts it, do not simply emerge from within an individual; they 'develop in the context of specific interactive episodes and contexts'. In the light of this thinking, you are encouraged to consider what underlying cultural, political and social assumptions you yourself may or may not bring with you into the room.
- Feminist theory, constructivist and postmodern thinking lends critical perspectives on narratives as they develop between the therapist and the client. Narratives are explored with reference to their cultural meaning and impact.
- Therapeutic practice is considered with reference to 'emancipatory' and 'critical' aspects. You are encouraged to reflect on the extent to which social and political considerations are compatible with ethical guidelines about neutrality and objectivity.
- 'Objectivity' is re-examined in the light of qualitative research and postmodern thinking, and it is suggested that even a stance of 'distance' is a deliberate, value-loaded stance.

THE POWER OF THE HELPING PROFESSIONS

We have already referred to the reactions to Freud from feminist thinkers. In this chapter, we will dig a little deeper into the issue of 'power' in the consultation room. As Guggenbuhl-Craig stresses, few can do more harm than those who act in the name of good. Together with social workers, nurses and teachers, counsellors and psychotherapists meet people at a very vulnerable and sometimes helpless stage in their lives. As discussed in the previous chapter, how we as individuals act in emotionally charged meetings is a complicated process. Ongoing reflection, feedback and support is needed in order to prevent us from enacting emotions or rushing to false or hasty conclusions.

This chapter revolves around our social responsibility as therapists. You are encouraged to consider what impact your assessments, conclusions and general input have on people at a more general, sometimes political, level. When we are in the thick of our own culture, it can often seem like a blur – a bit like when you fly through a cloud in an aeroplane.

POSTMODERNISM

To comprehend postmodernism, we need first to know about modernism, or modernity.

Modernity is an era characterised by technical and scientific progress. Technocracy is a concept linked to modernity, and it indicates how industrialisation resulted in technological innovation being elevated to an almost godlike status.

Certainty and progress became underpinning values for Western industrialised society where 'man' invented the train and travelled to the moon. Everything seemed possible. Mystery and ambivalence became quaint remnants from prior or other 'primitive' societies. The approach to life typical for modernity was that 'man' really could control everything, given time and resources. Indeed, Freud was a man of this time. Like his contemporaries, he strived for an all-inclusive explanation to life secrets that was simply waiting to be mapped out.

The Second World War became, in many ways, a turning point. With it came an economic vulnerability together with a gradual awareness that infinite progress could be ill-founded and, in fact, unrealistic. This new caution was heightened by the chilling illustration of the actual consequences of running the world like a factory. Hitler's social experiment spawned research into the dark side of affluent society. Some scholars who were in exile during the Second World War founded the Frankfurt Institute, which still today produces ground-breaking research in the area of modern and postmodern society. The Frankfurt Institute is a renowned multidisciplinary response to the need to understand modern society. Universal 'truth' was for the Frankfurt Institute a hallmark of fascism that had taken the technocratic developments that characterised modernity to an extreme. The thinkers coined the term 'critical theory'.

Adorno, Marcuse, Horkheimer and Fromm are some of the founders who instigated studies into 'authoritarian personality' in modern society, for instance. Marcuse advocated a 'liberation from the affluent society', suggesting that modernity caused weak egos and a massive social conformity, seducing people with the 'dream' of frictionless progress and, ultimately, general perfection. Marcuse expressed early fears that mass media, school, etc. would replace the family and that people would turn to herd-like conformity. The critical theory challenged modernity and progress in ways that have inspired Schön's thinking about technical rationality, which he regards as a threat to reflective practice. A well-known contemporary scholar from the Frankfurt Institute is Jürgen Habermas, who coined the phrase 'colonisation of our life world'. Habermas expands on the thinking of apolitical, materialistically orientated citizens 'bought' into silence by the convenience of modern-day standards. As we shall see in the next chapter, Habermas has been criticised for ignoring the fact that the standard of living does not include everyone. The idea of a 'faceless' society is ill founded, argue some; the comfortable living benefits primarily the same category in society that have always been comfortable, namely the white, middle-class man.

J-F Lyotard (1924–1998) was one of the first to use the concept postmodern, through his book *The postmodern condition* (1986). Lyotard addresses how modernity has rested on the belief that people could be 'run' and organised like machines. He developed thinking about 'narrative knowing' with which many postmodern and post-structuralist thinkers of today agree.

FROM 'UNIVERSAL' TO 'LOCAL' TRUTHS

Postmodernism reflects a reaction to the industrialised, modern society with its idea of a universal 'truth'. Kvale (1999: 32) refers to postmodernism as:

> *characterised by a loss of belief in an objective world and incredulity towards meta-narratives of legitimisation . . .*

Moving away from the belief in a universal will, general laws and history of nature, postmodern thinking explores people in their *local* context. *Narratives* have become a way of approaching this subject. Kvale (1999: 34) continues:

> *With the collapse of the universal meta-narratives the local narratives come into prominence . . . The local interaction, the communal network is the point of departure . . . There is today an interest in narratives, in the telling of stories . . . emphasising communication and the impact of a message upon an audience . . .*

Postmodernism reflects an interest in 'local' truths as opposed to universal truths, with certain parallels to what Schön refers with his concept frame-reflection. Things can look different, depending on 'where you are'. Winter et al. (1999: 181) recognise how Schön's theory arrived at a time when local and shifting, rather than dogmatic and universal, truths were relevant concerns to explore. Winter et al. conclude:

> *When a phrase catches on in the way that 'Reflective Practitioner' has done in the years since Donald Schön first published his book with that title in 1983, we can be sure that it has connected with something historically important.*

FUSION OF HORIZONS

The metaphor of the alchemic bath referred to in the previous chapter rests on the principle that not only the client but also the therapist brings something unique into the equation. This is the underlying thinking in narrative inquiry focusing 'local' truths and framings. The underlying constructivist thinking is central here. Meanings do not simply emerge from within an individual, they 'develop in the context of specific interactive episodes and contexts' (Crossley, 2000: 59). *What* we bring with us as practitioners into these interactive and formative episodes is important to consider; how a practitioner participates in making frames becomes the essential concern in reflective practice. Schön and Rein write (1994: 29):

> *Participants in [frame reflection] must be able to put themselves in the shoes of other actors . . . they must have the complementary ability to consider how their own frames may contribute to the problematic situations . . .*

As all forms of narratives are 'ambiguous representations' of a unique combination of experiences (Riessman, 1993), it is likely that we will never fully understand the words in the same sense as the teller or the author of the story does. We are 'subjected to the blindness' in the compartments of our life. Lacan (in Sarup, 1993: 13) illustrates the ambiguous meaning of language with the following tale:

> *A train arrives at a station. A little boy and a little girl, brother and sister, are seated in a compartment face to face next to the window through which the buildings along the station platform can be seen passing as the train pulls to a stop. 'Look', says the brother, 'we're at the Ladies!'; 'Idiot', replies his sister, 'Can't you see we're at Gentlemen?'*

Sarup comments:

> *Lacan seems to be saying: we are all sitting on one side of the compartment or the other: we are all subject to the blindness imposed by our seats in the compartments; there is no other way of being on the train.*
>
> (Sarup, 1993: 13)

A story undergoes changes when shared. To understand the other, we will have to change seats, so to speak – maybe move a bit back and forth. Hearing someone else – in the true sense often referred to in therapy – will involve a 'fusion of horizons' (Gadamer, 1989). This is a term usually connected to hermeneutics, sometimes described as the theory about interpretations, and we shall return to their meaning in Chapter 4. Ultimately, hermeneutics propose that all understandings are based on a co-production of understandings between the writer and the reader, the speaker and the listener. We fill the gaps between the lines, so to speak, with our own content.

KEY THINKER

Jacques Lacan (1901–1981)

Lacan started professional life as a forensic psychiatrist. In 1951 he instigated a private weekly seminar in Paris urging 'a return to Freud', with a particular focus on the linguistic nature of our collectively held symptoms of disease (symptomatology). His 27-year long series of seminars was influential in Parisian cultural life and has had a great impact on psychoanalytic theory and clinical practice in general.

As described in the example, Lacan regards the therapist and the client as two passengers facing different directions on a train and doubts that true mutual understanding is ever possible. People are unable to relate to each other without interpretations and misinterpretations as part of the process. Lacan (in Payne 1993: 47) concludes:

> *Psychoanalysis has only one medium: the patient's speech . . . there is no speech without a reply, even if it is met only with silence.*

Lacan focuses on 'defects and excesses':

> *Even when the temptation to fill the void [of silence] is resisted and the silence is maintained, it is too easy to misinterpret the silence . . . Far*

> *from celebrating speech and language for their creative, expressive, or healing potential, Lacan instead focuses on their defects and excesses.*

Postmodern thinking may, as Loewenthal proposes, have profound implications for therapeutic practice. For those who wish to explore post-modernism further, Loewenthal and Snell provide a comprehensive, in-depth source in their book *Post-modernism for psychotherapists*. Loewenthal and Snell (2003: 1) conclude:

> *The post-modern challenges the modernist assumptions that prevail in so much of psychotherapy, counselling, psychology and psychoanalysis. We suggest that in some important senses the work of psychotherapists . . . may be out of touch with current cultural practices and this is the world from which our patients/clients come.*

DISCOURSE AND NARRATIVES

Language enjoys a central role in postmodernism. Both discursive and narrative inquiries highlight how language shapes our sense of self and our understanding of others. Fook and Pease (1999: 14) write:

> *Discourse analysis examines the assumption, language and myths that underpin particular positions in order to show that discursive practices are ordered according to underlying codes and rules which govern what may be thought or said at any time.*

Foucault talks about 'what is possible to speak about' at certain times in history. Fook and Pease (1999: 14) suggest that a prevailing view is prominent 'because people are unaware of that it is only one of several possible alternative views'. They refer to Foucault, who defines discourse as 'historically variable ways of specifying knowledge and truth – what is possible to speak at a given moment' (cited in Fook and Pease 1999: 14). In this sense the concept 'discourse' refers to something larger than the meaning of words and stories conveyed between two people. Polkinghorne (1988: 31) writes: 'A discourse is an integration of sentences that produces a global meaning.'

An alternative concept for culturally available building blocks is the 'dominating narrative' (Lyotard, 1986). Feminist writers suggest that our dominating narratives within the therapeutic field still convey distinct features of a white, middle-class male society. Oedipal drama and penis envy are, however, examples of core concepts in psychoanalytic thinking that have undergone considerable postmodern critique, by feminists in particular, as addressed earlier in this book. Mitchell (2002) compares Freud's thinking on women to the 'oppression of a social class and regards them as barred from access to power and cited as proof of inferiority'.

There is, feminist scholars continue, a striking absence of women in the therapeutic discourse, and when references are made, they usually refer to old stereotypes. In her book about Lacan and post-feminism, Wright (2000: 14) critiques Klein's position of women 'in preordained social roles – daughter, wife, mother – within the restrictions of an inherited patriarchal circuit', and he seeks development in our way of referring to women:

> *Psychoanalysis is currently the only discourse offering a theory of the unconscious. Hence [to develop this thinking] has been, and still is, of crucial interest for feminists and indeed all those who want to place themselves outside the rigid definition of sexual differences.*

As Foucault highlights, when one discourse surrounds us and becomes so familiar that it is taken for granted, it can be difficult to see other options. The usage of words and sentences can be extremely important to consider as the client narratives develop through the therapeutic work. Kristeva's (1989) reference to pregnancy and to 'chorion', which relates to the membrane enclosing the foetus in the womb (Kristeva, in Payne, 1993: 168), is a refreshing addition to penis envy and the many other phallic concepts that have characterised therapeutic narrative schemes so far.

Jan Fook suggests that reflective practitioners embrace the idea of post-modern critical theory. Postmodern theory does not acknowledge the power struggle that still characterises our society. Fook and Pease (1999: 12) emphasise the 'critical', emancipatory potential of postmodernism and of reflective thinking of our own professional role and practice. They write:

> *Because of its acknowledgement of multiple realities, postmodernism is often criticised for drawing attention away from the notion of social justice and common experiences of oppression . . . [W]hat we call postmodern critical theory is concerned with political struggles against racism, sexism and colonialism.*

They highlight the potential of Foucault's reasoning:

> *The liberating potential of Foucault's notion of discourse is that it provides the possibility of creating alternative discourses and repositioning ourselves in the dominant discourse. Personal and social change comes about by unravelling the discursive power of dominant discourses and re-creating ourselves as the basis for collective politics of the future.*
>
> (Fook and Pease, 1999: 14)

WHAT IS A MEMORY?

Dan McAdams focuses on 'life histories' and the way we sequence events in our life into a coherent story. Like Lacan, McAdams highlights how misleading our language can be; not just for others but also for ourselves. We are often unaware of our own framing of events. Cultural values and beliefs play an important role here. So do our 'significant others' – our parents or carers. McAdams (1993: 11) refers to our stories as personal myths, which we 'tacitly, even unconsciously, composed over the course of [our] years'. He continues:

> *We are all tellers of tales. We seek to provide our scattered and often confusing experiences with a sense of coherence by arranging the episodes of our lives into stories. This is not the stuff of delusion or self-deception. We are not telling ourselves lies. Rather, through our personal myths, each of us discovers what is true and what is meaningful in our life.*

The philosopher Ricoeur refers to 'narrative commitment' in psychotherapy. This involves putting 'the tattered remains of our experiences' into coherent stories or accounts. This is, after all, suggests Ricoeur (1998: 252), what memories are about:

> *What is to remember? It is not just to recall certain isolated events, but to become capable of forming meaningful sequences and ordered connections. In short, to be able to constitute one's own existence in the form of a story where a memory as such is only a fragment of the story.*

This is highlighted by Polkinghorne (1988) too as he emphasises the impact of how we re-author the stories about ourselves:

> *Psychotherapy and narrative have in common the construction of a meaningful existence. When they come to the therapeutic situation, clients already have life narratives, of which they are both the protagonist and author. The life narrative is open-ended: future actions and occurrences will have to be incorporated into the present plot. One's past cannot be changed . . . However, the interpretation and significance of these events can change . . .*

Case study 3.1 Recreating memory

Consider Miriam's ideas about herself from the case study below. Miriam is 17 years old and has been referred by her GP to psychotherapy for anorexia.

'I've always been picky with food,' says Miriam during her first session with Sarah, 'Ever since I was a baby, really.'

Miriam looks small in the chair. Her protruding bones and sunken face contrast with her huge eyes. She lapses into silence. On her arms, Sarah notices lanugo hair. She notices hair on her neck and on Miriam's face, too.

'I've always been fat,' she ponders. She shakes her shoulders without looking up. 'But that's because I've been greedy. When I was a baby, I didn't want her milk . . . I wanted that milk, what's it called, you know the one with the pink bear on.' Miriam giggles.

'A formula milk?' asks Sarah.

'Yes, but not just any formula either! It had to be, oh what's it called again . . .?'

'How old where you then?'

'Oh, I don't know . . . well, I must have been a couple of months or so I guess.'

Silence.

'You are saying that you remember that far back?'

Silence.

'Well, no . . . I suppose . . .Well, my mum has told me.'

'So, she's told you about her difficulties in dealing with your needs as baby . . . that she found it hard to feed you?'

'I didn't give her any choice, did I? I was greedy, I told you.'

Silence.

'I suppose . . . It can't be really right that a three month old knows about different types of milk like that.'

'It's difficult imagining a baby being so . . . so specific.'

'Mmmm.'

Silence.

'I've always pictured myself a picky little devil . . .'

During the brief interaction above, Miriam recreates a memory of herself. The case study highlights, first, the impact that other people's 'stories' have on us and the way we perceive ourselves. Having heard from her mother that she was greedy as an infant, Miriam had held on to a construct about herself that surfaced in the interaction with her therapist and could be reconstructed. The case study also illustrates the powerful role that the therapist has in the process of deconstructing and reconstructing memories, values and beliefs about the self.

Narratives give form to shared beliefs and transmit values. It is an important term within postmodern thinking. Polkinghorne (1988: 14) refers to the significance of narratives on both a personal and a cultural level:

> *[N]arratives perform significant functions. At the individual level, people have a narrative of their own lives, which enables them to construe what they are and where they are headed. At the cultural level, narratives serve to give cohesion to shared beliefs and to transmit values.*

THE OBJECTIVE STANCE OF THE THERAPIST

To assist someone in their re-creation of memories without imposing one's own interests and agendas was something that Freud himself established as paramount in any therapeutic intervention. As far as his espoused theory was concerned, keeping one's own opinions and values outside the therapy room was an underpinning principle for therapeutic practice. Freud (1938/1959: 39) often emphasised the importance of 'not acting on the temptation of being a teacher, model or image to other people to make men into his own image', which would reduce therapy to a process of 'repeating the damage done by parents as they crushed their child's independence'.

Given his own emphasis on being objective, it is possible that Freud, in the present context, would be the first to regret his hearing of, for instance, Dora – Freud's female client referred to earlier who was concerned about being approached by her father's friend. Freud (in Gay, 1989: 184) wrote:

> *Instead of genital sensation which would certainly have been felt by a healthy girl under such circumstances, Dora was overcome by disgust.*

What Freud, presumably objectively, framed as Dora's 'repressed desire' towards a 'perfectly desirable, albeit a little older man' has later been construed as an example of what Mitchell refers to as an oppressing discourse. Michael Billig's critique of Freud's case expresses this 'postmodern' shift in framing:

> *Freud's role in the saga is being reassessed. He no longer appears as a passive listener and detached scientist . . . In the late twentieth century, the problem is no longer seen to be Dora's resistance to the male phallus, but has become Freud's assumption about women's desire . . . Scholars have debated whether psychoanalytic ideas should be rejected outright for their masculine assumptions of whether a reformulation is possible (see for example . . . [lists authors] . . .). These debates have led feminist scholars to look at the famous case studies in new ways . . .*
>
> (Billig, 1997: 1–2)

Other historic documents reflecting male doctors' perception of female clients' problems lend distressing illustrations of how emotions and stereotypical images have been interwoven in a highly oppressive manner.

KEY THINKER

Michel Foucault (1926–1984)

A thinker who is often labelled post-structuralist is Foucault. He is a philosopher and historian who examined the codes and concepts by which societies operate with a particular interest in the 'principles of exclusion'. It is, highlights Foucault, in the 'us' and 'them' distinction that a society defines itself. He was particularly interested in distinctions between the sane and the insane, the criminal and the law abiding, and he surveyed social attitudes about asylums, hospitals and prisons from the fifteenth century onwards. He argued, for instance, that since the disappearance of leprosy, madness had come to occupy the position of 'the excluded'; the ones we can 'lock away'.

Some of his most famous books are *Madness and civilisation* (1961), *The order of things* (1966), *The archaeology of knowledge* (1969), *Discipline and punish* (1975), and *History of sexuality*, three volumes (1976–1984).

The post-structural philosopher Michel Foucault explores implicit and explicit power in medical assessment over time, for instance, with regard to the historical development of 'hysteria'. Foucault's texts on *Madness and civilisation* (Foucault, 1984) throw a chilling light on to therapeutic practice, as he expands on the theme of mental health 'care':

> *It is thought that Tuke and Pinel opened the asylum to medical knowledge. They did not introduce science, but a personality, whose powers borrowed from science only their disguise, or at most their justification. These powers, by their nature, were of a moral and social order . . .*
>
> *Pinel cites the case of a girl of seventeen who had been raised by her parents with 'extreme indulgence'; she had fallen into a 'giddy, mad delirium without any cause that could be determined'; at the hospital she was treated with great gentleness, but she always showed a certain 'haughtiness' which could not be tolerated at the asylum; she spoke 'of her parents with nothing but bitterness'.*
>
> *It was decided to subject her to a regime of strict authority; the keeper, 'in order to tame this inflexible character, seized the moment of the bath and expressed himself forcibly concerning certain unnatural persons who dared oppose their parents and disdain their authority . . . she was henceforth soothed and could not sufficiently express her gratitude toward the keeper who had brought an end to her continual agitation, and had restored tranquillity and calmed her heart.'*
>
> (Foucault, 1984: 160–61).

Foucault's criticism of psychotherapy as a conveyor of values and beliefs about right and wrong, sane and insane, etc. under 'the pretence of being science', is a disturbing one to most therapists. Tuke and Pinel act on a moral and social order, writes Foucault, and he highlights through this the importance of considering the dyad of therapist and client in the context of time and place.

Power within the mental health sector is often 'inherent'; it is rarely explicit or easy to spot.

ACTIVITY 3.1

The social constructionist perspective explores how we are constructed by the society that we live in. It is linked to what we earlier described as critical reflexivity and critical constructivism. This perspective suggests that persons can be understood as functions of social practices and relationships; even emotions can be traced to our 'enmeshment' in society. Shame and pride are examples of emotions that may have cultural connotations.

The girl 'treated' by Tuke and Pinel is described as 'haughty'. 'Haughtiness' appears to sum up some important expectations of women. It seems to say something about social and moral preconceptions at the time. It is also used by Tuke and Pinel to pathologise the girl. 'Race', which nowadays is recognised as a value-loaded word, has hidden meanings that convey prejudices about one group being 'better' or 'worse' than another.

- Can you think of more examples of commonly held descriptions that capture and may reinforce expectations of groups or individuals in society?

ACTIVITY 3.2

Try to come up with some examples in medical history where the mind and the body have been perceived, portrayed and 'treated' in drastically different ways from how they are now.

THE CRITICALLY REFLECTIVE PRACTITIONER

Foucault's analysis suggests that we regard 'truth' as a relative concept. What is to be regarded as knowledge depends on the knower.

REFLECTION POINT

Schön refers to policy making as something that relies heavily on perceptions that are taken for granted. He compares the policy making around an urban housing situation with the gestalt figure that to some looks like an old lady and to others as a young woman. What is a home to some can come across as a 'tip' to others. In politics, this is important to consider.

- It is sometimes not until our attention is drawn to how differently the same thing can be perceived that we realise that there are more ways than one to look at things. How could this thinking apply to therapy, do you think?

Mental health practitioners enjoy a tremendous influence through their assessments of 'sane' and 'insane', 'rights' and 'wrongs', 'thinkable' and 'unthinkable'; these are powerful narratives that can result in confinement for some and ordain others with divine status, depending on time and place. Many 'diagnoses', argues Foucault, actually rest on moral and social values. Our thinking and our experiences are 'shaped' by what Foucault proposes as a 'repertoire of dominant narratives' (Foucault, in Dallos and Miell, 1996: 112).

As referred to earlier, in the context of 'discourse', culturally guided ways of organising meanings, i.e. the meta narratives and available 'building blocks' (Dallos and Miell, 1996) at the time, can be very restrictive to our way of thinking. To recognise just how embedded our thinking may be in cultural values and commonly held beliefs implies thinking 'outside the box' of time and culture. This is difficult; some argue that it is impossible – as suggested earlier with reference to the Chinese proverb 'the last one to know the water is the fish'.

Foucault's concept of *épistémè* describes a kind of 'epistemological unconsciousness' of an era. The configuration of knowledge in a particular *épistémè*, argues Foucault, is based on a set of fundamental assumptions that are so basic to that *épistémè* that it could be said to be 'invisible' to people operating within it.

However, in a similar way to how Freud attempted to make the unconscious conscious, Schön (1983: 310) proposes that simply by recognising that we may see the world through certain lenses opens up a new kind of awareness. By recognising the notion that other perspectives – other lenses – exist, something new is being grasped:

> *When a practitioner becomes aware of his frames, he also becomes aware of the possibility of alternative ways of framing the reality of his*

> *practice. He takes notes of the values and norms to which he has given priority, and those he has given less importance, or left out of account altogether.*

Fook (in White et al., 2008: 145) addresses an important 'emancipatory' side to reflective practice. She regards 'the capacity to question and change existing power relations' as essential in reflective practice. Fook says:

> *[T]he critically reflective practitioner develops (reconstructs) their own practice in inclusive, artistic and intuitive ways which are responsive to the changing (uncertain, unpredictable and fragmented) contexts in which they work; and in ways which can challenge existing power relations and structures.*

SO, WHAT IS 'ILLNESS'?

When 'illnesses' reflect an unfair treatment of a person, it can be argued that the problem lies with the system, be it a family or a society, rather than with the individual. This is the stance that the feminist psychoanalyst adapts to eating disorders, for example. Chernin (1994: xv) asserts:

> *The female body has a story to tell. In its hunger, its hidden shame, its shadowy sense of guilt, there is the still as yet not fully articulated indictment of our culture's treatment of women . . . [they] are not supposed to want to 'surpass their mothers'.*

Chernin's ideas were referred to earlier with regard to a 'missing chapter' in therapeutic literature. Her own eating disorder spawned systematic inquiry and research into literature about the relationship between mother and daughter. She found much about father and son – and, to some extent, daughter – but little in the area of how to surpass the mother. Breaking free and growing up is a natural part of life, yet for many girls, Chernin discovered, it is a conflict-ridden process. Chernin concludes that there is a silence, an absence of available narratives on the theme of how girls are to liberate themselves from their mothers and grow into mature adults in adult relationships. Within the field of eating disorders, there are, however, concerns that are noticed more frequently now. Case study 3.2 is based on Greenberg's work with an anorexic client. It highlights the importance of reflection-in-practice with its reflexive awareness of the clinician.

Case study 3.2 Jane

Jane is 17 years old and suffers from anorexia. Initially, the psychiatrist approaches the new case with a predominantly explanatory commitment guided by technical reflections:

> *The clinical picture is typical of anorexia nervosa according to both ICD 10 and DSMIV (restricting subtype). She [Jane] shows a purposive reduction in food intake . . . It is important to assess her serum electrolytes status since a hypocalcaemia alkalosis would suggest that she is secretly inducing vomiting . . . Although she has not accepted that she is emaciated and that she needs help . . . she admitted to a number of distressing feelings . . . Her parents will probably also support putting pressure on her to accept admission. The psychiatrist will need to be firm . . . admission under compulsory order might need to be considered.*
>
> (Greenberg et al., 2003: 106, 110)

This approach can be viewed with single-loop thinking in mind (see Figure 3.1):

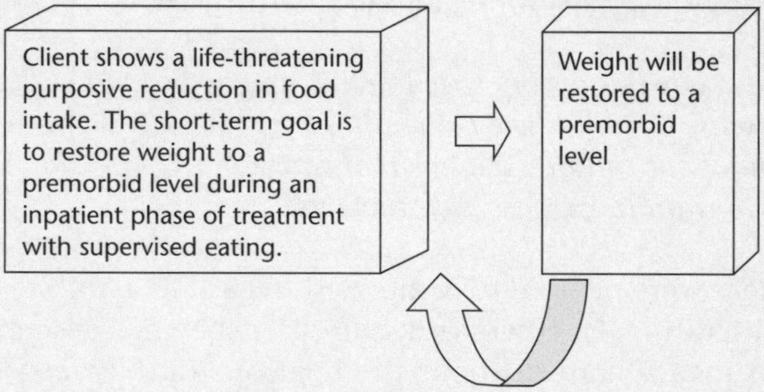

Figure 3.1: Single-loop learning about anorexia

Jane actually did gain weight after two months as an inpatient. However, soon after her discharge, she quickly lost weight again. In accordance with reflective practice, the unexpected outcome calls for a new hypothesis:

> *In the first three months of follow-up treatment the hypothesis that Jane's symptoms served a function in maintaining the current family system was explored.*

Greenberg et al. (2003: 112) continue with references that illustrate double-loop learning. The clinician reassesses the strategy and reformulates his hypothesis on the basis of a reflexive stance to Jane and the situation. This requires an ability by the male doctor to 'try on' the perspective and existence of Jane and her mother. The knowledge is transformed into practice with a new angle to the work with Jane:

> *It has become clear that both parents have had considerable difficulty in separating from their children . . . There is some evidence that [the mother] may have failed to come to terms with the divorce . . . Jane's mother now fears that Jane also will abandon her for her father . . . her mother would then have lost both daughters. These concerns for her mother might have been sufficient to cause Jane's relapse, particularly if coupled with an equal wish to be with her father . . . in fact, the illness has served as a tool to reconstitute the family . . . The father frequently returns now . . . The illness has also ended Jane's moves to establish independence from her mother. She has become clinging like a small child . . . who needs to be looked after, even fed. Sessions with Jane's mother supported the view that there was a marked interdependence between them and that this was a contributing factor to Jane's illness. Their relationship seemed to require Jane to be a 'little girl'.*

Greenberg et al.'s case study (2003: 108, 110) shows how we can expand on the single-loop learning about Jane with reflections that take her social family situation into account, as well as culturally transmitted values about women and their potential lack of power. Greenberg concludes:

> *The discussion above suggests that a variety of influences may be at work in shaping Jane's illness. These include factors understandable at physiological, psychological, interpersonal and socio-cultural levels.*

To bring in the therapist as a person, I have borrowed a quote from Finlay and Gough's book about reflexivity (2003: 11) that captures the human behind all our professional accounts. This personal, private reflection reminds us of the concerns raised in the previous chapter about Sarah's emotional response to her client. At the hub of the connection between the client and the therapist there is always a human being:

> *[Jane] and I are masters at intellectualising bulimia. Through our conversations, I have moved beyond the literal interpretation of bulimia as being only about thinness to thinking about how eating disorders also speak to personal longings. But it always has been hard for us to focus on emotional issues. I have come to see this as a relational problem to which we both contribute . . . Bulimia is about mess. Lisa and I talk about, study it, analyse it and WE DO IT! As perfectionists . . . we craft exteriors that contradict the mess in our lives. Still I know what goes on 'behind the closed doors' in Lisa's life, because I know what goes on behind my own closed doors.*

REFLECTION POINT

Consider the case study above. Viewed from a feminist stance, Lisa's eating disorder reflects her being trapped by expectations of women as caring, attractive daughters, mothers and wives.

- To what extent do you agree or disagree?

Fook emphasises the 'emancipatory' role of professionals. She suggests that the therapist, the social worker and the teacher have social and political roles to play. Where does this 'involvement' begin and where does it stop?

- How do we combine emancipatory requirements with being an objective listener?

ACTIVITY 3.3

Describe manhood or womanhood in your own words. Write for ten minutes, uninterrupted, starting with:

- Man/womanhood for me is . . .

Revisit your text with the following question in mind:

- What episodes in your life (experiences, encounters/relationships, reading, education, etc.) helped you to shape these definitions?

CHAPTER SUMMARY

The focus in this chapter has been on the 'critically reflecting' practitioner, with an interest in the 'emancipatory' aspects of reflective practice. The chapter brings the subject of 'power' into therapeutic practice and the area of mental health.

You have been encouraged to consider therapeutic practice in a political context, with reference to the following concepts.

- Fook (in White et al., 2008: 145) highlights the 'emancipatory' element of reflective practice, which involves 'the capacity to question

and change existing power relations' as essential in reflective practice: '[T]he critically reflective practitioner develops (reconstructs) their own practice in . . . ways which can challenge existing power relations and structures.'
- Postmodernism reflects a reaction to the industrialised, modern society with its idea of a universal 'truth'. Modernity is critiqued for its natural scientific, technical outlook on all areas of life, implying that people can be 'run' as efficiently as machines.
- Social constructionism 'replaces scientific objectivity with a conception of socially informed subjectivity' and explores how we are constructed by the society that we live in.
- Discursive and narrative inquiry capture how the basis of our thinking is expressed by words and situated in language.
- Narratives are both carriers and makers of personal and cultural values and beliefs.

SUGGESTED FURTHER READING

Gergen, M (1997) *Towards a new psychology of gender*. New York: Routledge.

This is quite complicated but worthwhile reading about gender in therapy. Mary Gergen writes from the assumption that men and women have different experiences, which generate different modes of thinking and relating. She explores how psychology and therapy may respond to, instead of ignoring, these differences.

White, M (1990) *Narrative means to therapeutic ends*. New York: Norton & Co.

White is the father of narrative therapy. He proposes that the problem for clients arises 'when the stories of their lives, as they or others have invented them, do not sufficiently represent their lived life'. White explores how therapy can be understood in terms of its narratives. This is a good introduction for those who want to learn more about therapy with a constructionist focus. White draws on Foucault and gives a historical background to a social constructionist thinking.

White, S, Fook, J and Gardner, F (2008) *Critical reflection in health and social care*. Maidenhead: Open University Press.

This is a selection of texts about critical reflection, and it includes accessible perspectives on most of the topics raised in this chapter. This is recommended reading for those who wish to go a little deeper into critical and emancipatory reflection.

CHAPTER 4

Understanding people

Theory and practice

CORE KNOWLEDGE

The emphasis in this chapter is on theory. You are encouraged to consider your theoretical framework in the light of basic beliefs and underlying values and assumptions.

- Theoretical frameworks will be explored in this chapter with reference to the concept 'epistemology'. This involves looking at the basic, underpinning beliefs from which we usually generate further knowledge.
- A central question posed in this chapter is whether therapy is a science or an art.
- Schön's distinction between an espoused theory and a theory-in-use is explored here with reference to conscious, integrative attempts or 'integration-in-practice'.
- Reflective therapeutic practice is explored in terms of a combination of an empathic, reflective understanding with a professional expert stance. We will look at what the philosopher Ricoeur refers to as a dialectic relationship between a 'narrative' and an 'explanatory' commitment to our clients' stories.

INTRODUCTION

This chapter examines theoretical frameworks. We will focus on therapeutic modalities and what basic values they may rest on. We will also explore other, more recent views of reflective practice, for instance that of Beverly Taylor, who suggests that we can think in terms of three different types of reflective practice – practical, technical and emancipatory. In Chapter 5, Dr Biljana van Rijn will expand on the principle of different types of knowledge and reflection as part of reflective practice.

EPISTEMOLOGY

Epistemology derives from the ancient Greek words *episteme* meaning 'knowledge' and *logos* meaning 'rational'. Epistemology is largely concerned with breaking down a potentially infinite ladder of beliefs and identifies patterns and structures in different inferences. Epistemology asks questions about the bedrock and the ultimate foundations of beliefs.

Narratives and basic values are linked, at times beyond our own awareness, on the basis that they are things that we have grown to take for granted. In our daily lives, knowledge holds a core position; it involves everything from our assumption that morning will follow night to concerns of a moral, political or religious nature. What we hold as 'evidence' (Cardinal at al., 2005: 11) is often based on 'inference' from one set of beliefs to another. Inference is the 'move that we make when we reason from one or more claims to a conclusion'.

Taylor (2006: 88) writes:

> *Epistemology concerns itself with knowledge generation and validation, meaning that it tries to ascertain how to make new knowledge and how to judge whether it is trustworthy and 'true'. Ontology is the meaning of human existence. These two main foci of human interest are related to each other if you accept the argument that knowing about human existence is the basis for knowing the answer to any questions humans might pose.*

IS THERAPY AN ART OR A SCIENCE?

The issue of knowledge in counselling and psychotherapy is linked to debate about whether therapy is a science or an art. What kind of basic beliefs do we actually infer 'evidence' from? Safran and Muran (1994: 223) emphasise the importance of acknowledging 'the tension between art and science':

> *The tension between art and science is a perennial one, and any claims to have resolved this tension in a definite way would be trivializing a profoundly difficult issue . . . Freud (cited in Gay, 1989: 185) once spoke about psychoanalysis as an 'impossible profession'. Psychotherapy research, with all its complexities and ambiguities, seems to us to be no less impossible. The challenge is to try to do clinically meaningful research in full awareness of these complexities and ambiguities.*

Sussman's perhaps slightly uncompromising conclusions are helpful when considering just how influential our basic beliefs about therapeutic practice can be. In the context of 'benevolence', Sussman (1992: 117) refers to a study of how therapy students perceive their professional future:

> *[Hammer discusses] differences between individuals who approach psychotherapy as a science and those who view it as an art. He states that the student who needs to identify with the role of an absolute scientist is usually one who needs to see himself as being powerful, masterful, intellectual, self-controlled and masculine, rejecting all traits of weakness, passivity and emotionality.*

Hammer found that the students who hoped to approach clients in the role of a scientist showed signs of 'using the discipline of science as a means of exerting control . . . and deny an underlying conviction of weakness and vulnerability'.

With a similarly unforgiving analysis of the student therapist who conceptualised their future therapeutic career as an art, Sussman quotes Hammer:

> *[T]he student who strongly identifies with the role of an absolute artist . . . tends to try to gain a feeling of personal superiority by trying to confirm an image of himself as someone who is tender, gentle, affectionate, emotional, sensitive, intimate, non-combative, aesthetic, altruistic. He identifies with all of these feelings as a value but does not really experience them or live them as a reality.*

These are harsh words. The way in which therapy students are stereotyped by Hammer places the therapist on a pedestal, somehow leaving very little room to be anything but 'perfect'. However, whether or not we experience ourselves as adhering to a science or an art actually does influence the way we gather information and reach conclusions.

As Taylor suggested, epistemology is linked to ontology. Redmond (2006: 5) reminds us that this is ultimately what frame reflection is about. She writes that it 'deals with acknowledging the meaning that individuals ascribe to their existence', or, as Schön (1983: 163) puts it: 'A practitioner's stance toward inquiry is his attitude towards reality with which he deals.'

DIFFERENT STANCES TOWARDS REALITY AND CLIENTS

Rowan and Jacobs (2003: 132) argue that beyond separate modalities there are common themes that unite different 'types' of therapists. Regardless of whether the therapist 'belongs' to a psychodynamic, humanistic or cognitive-behavioural theoretical camp, there are certain traits that transcend this. Rather than assessing therapy with regard to different modalities, Rowan and

Jacobs suggest that we look at the 'difference between their stances in terms of working as 'an instrumental therapist, the authentic therapist and the transpersonal therapist'. Rowan and Jacobs continue:

> *[The therapists' positions] create a greater difference perhaps than between orientations. They have different aims, different beliefs and different notions of self.*
>
> *In the **instrumental position** the client is usually regarded as someone who has the problem, which needs to be put right . . . Specific techniques have to be learned and put into practice in time-limited work, for example, which nearly always include identification of a clear focus or problem. The client is there to be cured . . . More or better techniques are the way forward, and to test these objectively is the main goal of research . . .*
>
> *In the **authentic position**, personal involvement is much more acceptable, with the therapist much more closely identified with the client and more openly concerned to explore the therapeutic relationship. The idea of the wounded healer is often mentioned as is the idea of personal growth . . .*
>
> *In the **transpersonal position**, the boundaries between therapist and client may fall away. Both may occupy the same space at the same time, at the level of what is sometimes termed 'soul', sometimes 'heart' and sometimes 'essence': what they have in common is a willingness to let go of all aims and all assumptions.*
>
> (Rowan and Jacobs, 2003: 6)

REFLECTION POINT

- Where would you position yourself with regard to Rowan and Jacobs's three different 'types' of therapists?

THE RELATIONSHIP

In spite of rigorous research there is, as Tudor-Sandahl, writes, 'no curing factor as such' found in therapy. Much research suggests, however, that the *relationship* is the most important aspect of counselling and psychotherapy. The psychoanalyst Janet Malcolm thinks that the 'impossibilities' involved in talking therapies are consistent with what people come to therapy for in the first place – namely, that life itself is pretty impossible. Human life is immensely complicated. We may never, as the existentialists address, fully understand life. There is also the dilemma of memory and what Bion referred to as 'constant conjunction'. We store experiences and call upon prior knowledge to orientate ourselves in the present, both for good and for bad. Freud always argued that there were several people in the consultation room, each person conveying voices representing the values and beliefs of significant others from the past. Counselling and psychotherapy can, many argue, offer a rare and important reflective space for addressing human life on its own terms. In her book *Psychoanalysis: the impossible profession*, Malcolm (1981: 6) writes:

> *The phenomenon of transference – how we all invent each other to early blueprints – was Freud's most original and radical discovery . . . The concept of transference at once destroys faith in personal relations and explains why they are tragic: we cannot know each other. We must grope around for each other through a dense thicket of absent others.*

Psychodynamic thinking implies that our past often obscures our present. We fail to hear what people 'really' are saying; we read in meanings that may not always be there. We 'grope around', as Malcolm puts it, through the 'thicket of absent others'.

VIRTUAL WORLDS

Long before the internet monopolised the concept 'virtual', Schön spoke about psychotherapy offering people 'virtual worlds'. Schön (1983: 161) refers to psychotherapy as a place where feelings and experiences can be explored at a pace and in a way that ordinary life seldom allows for:

> *Actions which might be otherwise irreversible can be examined for their meanings, revised and tried again . . . [T]he therapist must become adept at converting his relationship with the patient into a world of inquiry in which thoughts and feelings can be seen as sources of discovery rather than as triggers to action . . .The therapist's ability to use the transference as a virtual world depends on his ability to read its signs.*

Schön (1983: 118) writes about 'transference as an object of shared inquiry'. He uses transference in terms of a space, the virtual space, in which the client can experiment:

> *The patient has an interest in repeating the past in the present, which leads him to transfer messages from outer life situations to the therapeutic one . . .*

ACTIVITY 4.1

Therapy as a virtual world

Read the following case study about Moira with the concept of a 'virtual world' in mind. Both Moira and Schön refer to the psychodynamic concept of 'transference' as a means to work through emotions.

- How could the principle of 'virtual world' translate into your practice and modality?

Case study 4.1 Moira

I actually used to say to my partner at first that 'my therapist is mad as a hatter!' Our first session seemed surreal. She sat there all quiet and I thought what's this all about? Then, gradually, I felt both freer and safer than I've ever done before.

It was as if anything goes. Not in a bad way, but in a warm, safe, loving kind of way. Sometimes I'd walk out of some sessions with roaring laughter ringing in my ears and we would have laughed together. With hindsight, I think that she might just have smiled or maybe just chuckled. I think that I often read in reactions . . . transference, I guess.

In the beginning I'd come home and say my therapist said this and that 'She says that you should look after me more' or 'She says that I've had a really hard childhood'. But, really, most of the time, she actually just gave me space to say those things! To connect, I suppose, to all those needs that I didn't even know that I had. She would perhaps nod, maybe sometimes agree. But she probably just said a fraction of what I felt she did. She did feel very present, though, very real. She still does. I do feel that she was so much on my side. I feel accepted by her and that's a feeling that I can return to when I need to. It was a very special experience of being . . . well, of being special, I suppose (laughter). Sometimes it felt like I'd sat in her lap crying my eyes out. It was like she had stroked my hair. She never did that, of course, but she might as well have done . . . because that's what it felt like.

I'd never experienced anything like that before, and it made me warm and fuzzy just thinking about it between the sessions. I really felt that my therapist cared and that I mattered to her. Each session was different. Sometimes I was tired, and I would lie down on the couch instead of sitting in the armchair. 'What if I fall asleep?' I remember asking. She said she'd wake me in time if I did. 'But if you need to sleep, you shall sleep,' she said. I had a feeling that anything I would do would be okay with her. That was such a new thing for me. I can't begin to tell you how different that felt!

But, it did surprise me, at least in the beginning, how strict she'd be with the time! There we were, kind of swirling around one minute in the open space with thoughts and feelings that I didn't even know existed before. A kind of 'crazy' world, it felt at first, on the one hand. Then – 'time's up, right, that's it!'

I couldn't believe it at first. I used to start things up just before we'd end just to see . . . you know, to see if she wouldn't forget about the time. But she wouldn't. That was the one thing that never changed!

In the beginning it felt like we had our own little world, a separate world. It was so different to what I was used to. I used to have a feeling of having gone out in space with her. But, after precisely fifty minutes – not even once fifty-five, or even fifty-one minutes, it was as if she turned off the engine on our space shuttle and said 'Right, time to get out'.

But do you know what? It was precisely because of this, I realised afterwards, that I could feel so free with her in the sessions. I knew that we wouldn't sail off into chaos – like we had in my family with my mum drinking and all that. It was those boundaries – the same time and the same place and all that – that made it all so safe. And that she'd let me speak and think freely, of course. To me, she kept her promise; I could rely on her, trust her. She allowed me to be who I really was, but she also kept to some of those really basic things. The last thing I wanted was to run riot in the open space. That was what my whole childhood had been about. Chaos. She gave me a completely different experience of the world. I will always carry that with me.

REFLECTION POINT

How do you react to Moira's account?

- Compare your own experience of counselling or psychotherapy to Moira's, with regard to boundaries and the content of the session. What type of therapy suits you? Why?
- What other ways are there to work with 'virtual worlds' and offer the client space to explore emotions and relationships safely?

KNOWING 'RIGHT' FROM 'WRONG'?

The psychoanalyst Bion (1962: 7) stated that:

> *[i]n psychoanalytical methodology the criterion cannot be whether a particular usage is right or wrong, meaningful or verifiable, but whether it does or does not promote development.*

As described earlier, 'categories' such as anxiety should not, writes Schön, be confused with a 'case of anxiety' in the sense that physicians might infer a case of chickenpox or mumps.

Knowing right from wrong brings us back to the question of what counsellors and psychotherapists are actually meant to contribute with.

Bion also famously suggested that the therapist should enter each session 'without memory and desire', which sounds like a contradiction to the idea that framing is inevitable. Bion understood the challenge for human beings in terms of how we can think for ourselves. How do we become our own subjective being? How do we 're-learn' to think for ourselves, rather than acting and thinking on the basis of what others may prefer? These were key questions underpinning psychotherapy, according to Bion. He referred to the analyst's proper stance as one of 'reverie', with the overriding aim of tuning into the client rather than being preoccupied with theories or one's own thoughts, e.g. without one's own memory and desire. Yet, Bion too had his 'markers'. Bion (1962: 35) conceptualised memories as 'undigested facts', which he labelled beta-elements. He used the term alpha function to describe a process analogous with digestion that aims to transform emotions into 'personal possessions rather than facts'.

'CAUSE AND EFFECT'

The link between alpha and beta elements was understood, by Bion, in the context of the philosopher Hume's thinking about cause and effect. We expect, for instance, that the sun will rise in the morning because we have experienced that two events such as sunrise and morning go together frequently enough. Hume described this as a 'constant conjunction' rather than as a necessary connection. If something follows an event frequently enough, our belief in this connection grows, and we are led to create a necessary connection in our minds. We begin to speak of the first event as 'causing' the second event while, in fact, reasoned Hume, cause is more a feature of human psychology.

Bion's idea of 'reverie' involved a psychoanalytic stance focusing early object relations, tracing dysfunctional relationships back to infancy. Bion used the term 'listening breast' in relation to the therapist (Bion, 1962). Many therapists from other modalities distance themselves from an overriding focus on regression in therapy. As suggested earlier, the existential therapist rejects the idea that clients need to regress and revisit-through-experience previous relationships in order to achieve deep change. However, like their psychodynamic and cognitive-behavioural colleagues, Existential therapists usually adopt a stance where they hope to gain insight into the unique subjective experience of the client. Yalom writes:

> *The . . . existential analysts must approach the patient's phenomenology; that is, he or she must enter the patient's experiential world.*
>
> (Yalom, 1980: 17)

PHENOMENOLOGICAL FRAMING

The prospect of entering someone's experiential world is by definition an act of 'non-framing'. In very simple terms it involves suspending the beliefs that we ordinarily hold and take for granted. For a therapist it becomes rather a matter of surrendering, or letting go of their own frameworks of understanding – with a view to 'stepping into the client's shoes', as Schön puts it. Merleau-Ponty (1999: 200) draws our attention to the 'merging' that can take place in dialogue that rests on intersubjectivity:

> *In the experience of dialogue, there is . . . a common ground . . . a dual being, where the other is for me no longer a mere bit of behaviour in my transcendental field, nor I in his . . . Our perspectives merge into each other, and we exist through a common world.*

Child psychiatrist Daniel Stern offers an illustrative example of a phenomenologically inspired closeness through the so-called 'kairos moment' which he believes captures qualitative shifts in therapy. Based on his experience of infants' and young children's interaction with care givers, Stern has observed the impact of brief moments during the course of interaction where 'each person intuitively partakes in the experience of the other'.

THE 'PRESENT MOMENT'

Stern (2004: 169) refers to the 'present moment' to describe this intersubjective experience:

> *Take, for example, the patient who suddenly sat up to look at her therapist. Right after the patient also sat up, the two found themselves looking at each other intently. A silence prevailed. The therapist, without knowing exactly what she was going to do, softened her face slowly and let the suggestion of a smile form around her mouth. She then leaned her head slightly and said 'Hello'. The patient continued to look at her. They remained looking in a mutual gaze for several seconds. After a moment, the patient lay down again and continued her work on the couch, but more profoundly and in a new key, which opened new material.*

THE POWER OF RELATIONSHIPS

The jointly lived and mentally shared experience, as described in terms of a present moment, requires that the therapist, to some degree, surrenders their framework of understanding and in the process abandons their 'technically accepted response'. Stern continues:

> *The nature of a now moment usually demands something beyond a technically acceptable response: It demands a moment of meeting . . . It must be spontaneous and must carry the therapist's personal signature, so to speak . . .*

The immense impact of this kind of connection has long been addressed within psychotherapy. Rogers (1961) and Buber (1947/1971) both wrote about the impact of moments when 'deep realness in one meets a realness in the other'. Rogers (1995: 8) referred to the term 'deep hearing', which captures the essence of phenomenologically shared moments. Here, otherwise separate experiences and perspectives are shared, and people bond beyond the usual boundaries within a society where competing with each other becomes the norm. Rogers writes:

> *When a deep realness in one meets a realness in the other, a memorable 'I–Thou relationship,' as Martin Buber would call it, occurs. Such a deep and mutual personal encounter does not happen often, but I am convinced that unless it happens occasionally, we are not living as human beings.*

Within psychoanalysis, object relations theory approaches the principle of 'unconditional regards', as Rogers calls it, with specific reference to our very earliest relationship in life. 'There is no such thing as a baby – only a nursing couple', concluded Winnicott when addressing infants as they developed in response to their care givers' actions. Bion often regarded the role of the therapist as to repair what the mother failed to do, namely to:

> *detoxify projected feelings, such as pain, fear of death, envy and hatred . . . and then return them in such a way that the [client] gets back good feelings of being held and understood rather than the original bad projection.*
>
> (Holmes and Bateman, 2002: 40)

Stern's research about the present moment coincides with a development within neuroscience in which natural science and phenomenology seem to strike up a somewhat unexpected relationship.

Research summary

Neuroscience + psychotherapy = neuropsychoanalysis

A 'fourth wave' in object relations

Object relations theory involved a view of the therapist as 'a receiver for infant and childhood communications'. Bollas (1987: 9) continues:

> *A patient does not simply represent his internal world to the analysts in narrative. He uses the analyst as a transference object and this usage if further articulated through the analyst's countertransference.*

Margareta Broden (2005: 83) refers to Stern's way of addressing the relationship as a vehicle for change in the mental organisation in terms of a 'fourth wave':

> *All schools of individual psychotherapy are based on a developmental theory . . . there is a need to understand present problems within a developmental context . . .*
>
> - ***Freud's drive theory represents the first wave.*** *The infant was described as being totally dominated by its biological instincts [with] little or no ability to interact.*
> - ***Anna Freud and the development of ego-psychology is the second wave*** *and was the first to focus interest on children.*
> - ***[T]he third wave is represented by object relations theory,*** *which brought the early mother–child relationship into focus.*
> - ***The 'fourth wave'*** *came out of object relations theory, but was also inspired by self-psychology, systems theory and cognitive theory. Infant psychiatry, or infant mental health, became a new multidisciplinary field . . . from a diversity of fields [including] sociology, anthropology and linguistics. The object relations school was now criticised for defining 'the other' in a relationship as 'an object'. Then there was a move towards concepts of 'subject–subject' in the process of mutual interaction and relationship development.*

As we shall see, neuroscience brings an interesting biological set of 'evidence' on to the scene, where references to phenomenologically shared moments fail to fit in with modern society's evidence requirements. Schore (2008: 23) refers to this as a 'dialectic between maturing organisms and the changing environment'. Schore continues:

> *Recent [integrative] models view . . . influences from the social environment as imprinted into the biological structures that are*

maturing during the early brain growth spurt, and therefore have long-enduring psychological effect . . . In a recent neuropsychoanalytic contribution I contend that . . . the structural maturation of the right brain is directly influenced by the attachment relationship.

REFLECTION POINT

- What evidence do you rely on to sustain your faith in counselling and psychotherapy?

INTEGRATION-IN-PRACTICE

Holmes and Bateman (2002: 4–6) refer to 'integration-in-practice' as a conscious choice of integrating models and theoretical frameworks. They use the term 'integration-in-practice' for integrative methods that have grown out of 'reflection-in-practice'.

Integration in psychotherapy involves the 'welding together of different strands into a new and coherent whole', either to emphasise or synthesise common factors under 'one common rubric'.

O'Brien and Houston (2005) offer integrative thinking with knowledge guided towards 'how to be' rather than 'what to do' with the client. They comment upon the dilemma involved in 'finding oneself doing things differently from one's original training'. This can cause a sense of disloyalty, observe O'Brien and Houston. But like Holmes and Bateman, they highlight a tendency among experienced therapists to integrate-in-action. O'Brien and Houston (2005: 19) write:

Experiments show, for example, that when senior practitioners' work with clients is recorded, it is not possible to tell what theoretical base each one is working from. It looks as if they are responding to the immediacy of the person in front of them, in the context of their long clinical experience, and this process has begun to sound interestingly similar.

REFLECTION POINT

Holmes and Bateman distinguish between three types of integration; organisational, theoretical and practical:

First, therapy may be organised so that different types of treatment are offered simultaneously or sequentially to a patient . . .

A second meaning – 'integration in theory '– refers to hybrid therapies . . . which explicitly bring together elements from other known therapies into new free-standing psychological treatment with their own methods and evolving traditions . . .

A third facet of integration in psychotherapy – which might be referred to as integration in practice – refers to the flexibility which is to be found in the practice of mature clinicians, whatever their basic training, in which they often consciously or unconsciously bring in elements of technique or theory borrowed from other disciplines.

- Do you ever integrate theories deliberately? If so, under which category would you place your type of integration?

CRITICAL CONSTRUCTIVISM

Constructivism has been referred to earlier in this book with reference to the assumption that we access reality through 'maps' of it. As Smith (1985) proposed, we are involved in making these maps all the time. Weaver (2008: 2) writes:

> *Constructivist psychotherapists work from the principle that there is more than one true judgment of the world. There is no kind of absolute authority to whom we can turn that will provide 'The Answer' . . . constructivism is about how people co-create dynamic personal realities . . . This means that our epistemology, our study of how we know what we know, is ever changing.*

How does this translate into our everyday practice? We return to the issue of basic belief to answer that question.

TO BE OR TO DO? THAT IS THE QUESTION

Whether we regard our role as being with the client or doing something to them, it involves a choice between two different epistemological positions. The philosopher Scruton (1996: 243) writes:

> *We may contrast two modes of understanding: science, which aims to explain appearances, and 'intentional understanding' which aims to*

> *interpret them . . . i.e. to describe, criticise and justify the human world . . . embedded in feeling and activity.*

The 'authentic' therapist approaches others with a participatory, 'intentional' understanding in mind, rather than with a scientific explanation. Carl Rogers (1961: 332) captures the idea behind 'intentional understanding', with his views on 'listening to understand'. He refers to an 'understanding *with* the person and not *about* him':

> *[To] listen with understanding . . . means to see the expressed ideas and attitudes from the other person's point of view, to sense how it feels to him, achieve his frame of reference to the things he is talking about.*

This is a type of reflection that the neo-Kantian philosopher Wilhelm Dilthey (1833–1911) coined in German as *Verstehen*. It is a mode of understanding that is guided towards interpretation as opposed to explanation, or *Erklärung*, as it was labelled by Dilthey.

We can either look at people as biological outcomes or as interactive beings, argued Kant in his theory on freedom. Intentional understanding responds to the idea that reality is linked to our perception and experience of it – similar to Smith's proposal with regard to the assumption that there is a reality that we can only access through our own experience. As Kant said:

> *There is no doubt at all our knowledge begins with experience . . . But although all our knowledge begins with experience, it does not follow that it arises from experiences.*
>
> (Kant, 1781/2007: 2)

FRAMING AS A MATTER OF 'JUDGING' THE SITUATION

Kant's attempts to straddle empiricism with rationalism paved the way for a new thinking on our own input into 'truths'. His attention to 'judgements' (Kant, 1781/2007: 97) has had important consequences. 'All acts of understanding can be referred back to judgements' wrote Kant. This belief plays an important role in many areas today, for instance in research where researchers are increasingly expected to 'own' their questions. Finlay and Gough write:

> *We realise that meanings are negotiated within particular social contexts so that another researcher will unfold a different story . . . we no longer seek to abolish the researcher's presence . . . researchers no longer question the need for reflexivity: the question is [now] 'how to do it'.*

As suggested earlier, the way we 'judge' situations influences how we 'construct' our maps of 'reality' and events. This is usually at the very heart of counselling and psychotherapy. For a client, a trauma may have occurred. Yet, as Bion (1962) proposes, it is not the past in itself that matters; it is the trace it leaves in our presence that therapy usually revolves around. We tend in this sense to give 'judgement' a precedent role to actual, undeniably real, scientifically evidenced events.

We looked at the idea of 'reality' as something that can be reconstructed through negotiating new meanings, or 'judgements' as Kant would say. Social constructionism, as proposed by Gergen, emphasises how these new meanings take form in relation to others. Even 'realities' such as death can be reconstructed in the light of how the meaning of the actual bereavement is being negotiated between people, with their personal and cultural 'baggage' in mind. The psychoanalyst Symington echoes this thinking when he explores 'reality' and 'truth' in therapy as something that exists in between the persons seeking it:

> *Truth does not exist as some external idea, as Plato thought, but as a reality that exists in between; in between two persons seeking it.*

RESEARCH ABOUT 'HEARING' OTHERS

What Rowan and Jacobs referred to as the instrumental positioning of a therapist could be argued to be related to the *Erklärung* view on 'reality'. This is, as suggested, usually anchored in natural sciences. People are approached as 'one of a kind' rather than with an interest in their unique experiences. The *Erklärung* model often relates to an 'average' version of 'man' that can be explored in terms of deviations from commonly held denominators. This kind of approach to clients often rests on laboratory tested data, presented through quantitative data with tables, diagrams and easily accessible and shared information. One distinct advantage with this kind of information is that it is easier to validate by others. It can more readily be 'independently observed and verified [so that] there is a broad consensus as to its contents', which Davies (2004) flagged up as important criteria for evidence-based practice.

DIFFERENT GROUPS WITHIN THE SAME CAMP

So far, we have talked about a division between 'explaining' and 'understanding'. There is, however, a distinction within the *Verstehen* camp as well. There are many accessible and comprehensive books about research. John McLeod's *Qualitative research in counselling and psychotherapy* (2001) is highly recommended. McLeod (2001: 58) concludes that within qualitative research there are two somewhat opposing stances:

> *Phenomenologists argue that their method of 'bracketing' allows them to lay aside existing interpretive frameworks . . . From a hermeneutic perspective, by contrast, the basic argument is that to be human is to live in an 'interpreted world', a world in which experience is constructed in terms of language.*

INTERPRETIVE REFLECTION

Schön's theory about reflective practice rests on the belief that 'framing' is inevitable, which anchors the thinking within the hermeneutic, interpretive framework. However, Schön's emphasis on 'stepping into the shoes of the client' involves a phenomenological aspect where the practitioner 'suspends his own understanding', as Schön puts it.

Reflective practice can be compared with what in hermeneutics is called 'appropriation', which the philosopher Ricoeur describes as an act of rendering. When we read or hear someone else's account, we invariably add a new layer of understanding to the original account through our own 'framing'.

Traditionally reserved for scriptural interpretations, hermeneutics are now applicable to 'any human action' (Ricoeur, in McLeod, 2001: 21). A hermeneutic appropriation expects the reader or the listener to immerse themselves in someone else's accounts, which requires 'letting go' of one's own understandings of something. Ricoeur calls this a 'narrative commitment', where we follow the other – literally walking in their shoes – for an insight into where the other 'comes from'.

This kind of 'merging' (Ricoeur, 1998: 270) with others' understanding can almost be compared with Jung's alchemic bath, referred to earlier in the case study about Sarah and Pat. The story-teller's and the listener's individual understandings will mix like two chemicals and result in a new, third component. New understandings will be reached through a 'fusion of horizons'. Gadamer (1989: 269) defines horizon as follows:

> *The horizon is the range of vision that includes everything that can be seen from a particular vantage point . . .*

Our own horizon becomes 'illuminated' through an appropriation. A 'hermeneutic hearer' changes themselves in the process of 'listening to understand', as Rogers puts it. McLeod (2001: 28) concludes that:

> *The criterion for a satisfactory hermeneutic understanding . . . involves a transformation of the initial positions . . . in a 'fusion of horizons' or consensus over meaning.*

This highlights what Schön (1983: 163) refers to as 'considering our own marks'. How does our own framing impact on the situation?

> *Through his transaction with the situations, [the practitioner] shapes it and makes himself a part of it. Hence, the sense he makes of the situation must include his own contribution to it. Yet he recognises that the situation, having a life of its own distinct from his intentions, may foil his projects and reveal new meanings.*

Ricoeur (1998: 18) captures this responsibility when he elaborated on the hermeneutic concept of 'appropriation':

> *To appropriate . . . means 'to make one's own' what was initially 'alien', so that 'interpretation brings together, equalises, renders contemporary and similar. The act of appropriation does not seek to rejoin the original intentions of the author, but rather to expand the conscious horizons of the reader by actualising the meaning of the text.*

NARRATIVE AND EXPLANATORY COMMITMENT

Dilthey regarded explaining (*Erklärung*) and understanding (*Verstehen*) as conflicting forms of reflection. Only the latter was suitable for understanding people, he argued. *Erklärung* and *Verstehen* do indeed rest on two different basic beliefs about reality and how to generate knowledge. Scientific reflection rests on 'control'. It is about being one step ahead of the situation to predict outcomes and events by recognising patterns of a cause and effect nature. Interpretive understanding, i.e. a *Verstehen*-related stance, takes into account that psychological realities are messy. Our understandings are coloured by 'judgements' and we are restricted to language for sharing our experiences with others. We have already explored language with reference to Lacan's and Polkinghorne's ideas about the ambiguity involved in language.

Jürgen Habermas is a neo-Kantian contemporary philosopher who has pursued Dilthey's distinction with an interest in combining *Verstehen* and *Erklärung*. He reiterates the idea of language as both conveyor and creator of maps:

> *Narrative practice not only serves trivial needs for mutual understanding among members trying to co-ordinate their common task; it also has a function in the self-understanding of persons . . . [People] can develop personal identities only if they recognise that the sequences of their own actions form narratively presentable life histories; they can develop social identities only if they maintain their membership in social groups by way of participating in interactions in ways where they are caught up in the narratively presented histories of collectives.*
>
> (Habermas, 1987: 136)

Habermas has coined the phrase 'communicative rationality'. The term 'rational' suggests that something 'can be criticised or defended by the persons involved, so that they are able to justify them' (Giddens, 1988: 99). Habermas's project involved defending the 'rational' side of *Verstehen*, or as Giddens puts it, complementing 'cognitive-instrumental rationality' with a conception of 'communicative rationality'.

The postmodern thinker Lyotard (1986) criticises Habermas for imposing a scientific order to *Verstehen* in the process. We are, says Lyotard, in this way submitting to the terms set by a society where science and technology determines not just the way we talk about machines but also the way we construe people.

Symington (1986) draws our attention to the particularly ambiguous representations involved in therapeutic interpretations; we deal with aspects such as beliefs, dreams and hallucinations. As described earlier, Symington emphasises that the 'truths' about human beings' inner lives rest on a very different kind of 'truth' from that normally perceived within natural sciences with its tangible, generalising and measurable categories of knowledge.

Polkinghorne (1988: 179) talks about 'narrative truth' and reminds us that the point of psychotherapy 'is not to lead the analysand to create literal descriptions of or to recover past events. Instead, the past is to be reconstructed in the light of the client's present awareness'.

Critical hermeneutics help to combine the two types of outlook on the world; Paul Ricoeur describes it as a 'dialectical relationship' (see Figure 4.1) where one sparks off something new in the other.

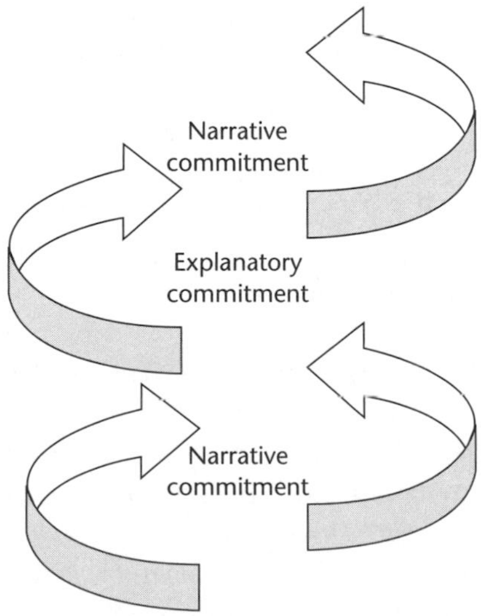

Figure 4.1: Ricoeur's dialectical relationship

Dialectics involves building on the dynamic quality of contradictions in the hope of reaching further development. It involves 'the back-and-forth interplay of opposing ideas' (Carter and Gradin, 2001: 5).

Schön too proposes a combination of being open to the unique while remaining anchored, professionally. He refers to this shift between different positions in terms of being open like a child together with an ability to perform systematic enquiries like a scientist. This requires working with 'a double vision' (1983: 132, 164). The inquirer must be open while at the same time able to impose an order of his own:

> *[The reflective practitioner] conducts an experiment in framing the problematic situation but 'he must recognise that he can always break it open later, indeed must break it open later in order to make sense of his transaction with the situation . . . The process spirals through stages of appreciation, action and re-appreciation.*

The practitioner is expected to 'make use of the experience he has accumulated in his practice [with] familiar categories of theory and techniques'. He will, in other words, not simply 'invite the client into a black box', concludes Schön. At the end of the day, we hope to offer some kind of expertise.

CLOSENESS AND DISTANCIATION

Critical hermeneutics lend us a framework that captures how therapists can move between 'merging' with their client and an interpretive, explanatory and more distant stance. Ricoeur (1970: 386) explores this approach to intersubjectivity in terms of a 'dialectic of presence and absence'. The therapist attempts to immerse themselves in the other's 'world' and will occasionally retract into their own, separate, understanding of the situation.

Critical hermeneutics help us to view an 'explanatory' stance as a complementary commitment to the narrative commitment, typical in interpretive-hermeneutic reflection (Sherwood in Ricoeur, 1970). Our understanding can benefit from moving back and forth between *Verstehen* and *Erklärung*, argues Ricoeur. This takes us between:

- 'closeness', with the aim of merging with the other's understanding; and
- 'distanciation', with a focus on explaining through 'law like statements' (Ricoeur, 1998: 269) based on identified framings.

This distanciation becomes an 'expert'-related stance that can be informed by different types of framings. Critical hermeneutics can be 'nourished by almost any form of inquiry' (Steele, 1989).

A rather extreme example of a critical hermeneutic study is Bärmark and Nilsson's (1983) study of the deceased Poul Bjerre, who was the first therapist to introduce psychosynthesis to Sweden. Bärmark and Nilsson describe how they at first approached Bjerre from a heroic, idolising stance. The stage of 'closeness' guided by an aim of 'surrendering' to Bjerre's world involved staying in Bjerre's house. They lived there for several weeks, tracing Bjerre's daily habits and routines – even to the extent of sleeping in his bed. The aim was to 'walk in Bjerre's shoes' as much as possible. In hermeneutic terms, this is called 'deep reconciliation' and has an almost ethnographic quality to it, motivated by the aim of seeking the experience 'as lived' by the other. Bärmark and Nilsson (1983: 19) write:

> *[At first] we applied a hermeneutic of deep reconciliation; we tried to understand Bjerre's reality like it could have been seen by himself.*

The next step in a critical hermeneutic inquiry is 'doing away with idols' and becoming critically aware of our own involvement, whether as researchers, readers or listeners. Bärmark and Nilsson describe it in terms of challenging one's own original infatuation. In their study, they turn their attention to their own underlying personal material; they explore what they might project on to the project in terms of their own wishes, fears and constructs. They question their own initially idealised view on the research subject. The original 'idolisation' is gradually replaced with 'suspicion' (Bärmark and Nilsson, 1983: 21), which often involves a growing awareness of one's own projections and 'tinted' lenses:

> *we [then] took the step toward the hermeneutics of suspicion. We could no longer take Bjerre's words [or our own involvement] for granted . . . We had to go beyond what was formulated in the texts in order to fill the gaps and explain the contradictions.*

Eventually they re-examine Bjerre's public document with a psychoanalytic theory as their 'framing', i.e. as their lenses through which they interpret his work. As suggested, this involves stages of closeness as well as inward journeys focusing their own involvement in the research.

Hermeneutic and narrative inquiries are, in this sense, rather complex communicative adventures between two personal stories, something that Ricoeur (Ricoeur, 1998: 15) refers to as the 'miracle' of discourse – a miracle involving the yearning to overcome the fundamental solitude of each human being. Ricoeur writes:

> *People do actually speak to one another . . . Why? Because being-together, as the existential condition for the possibility of any dialogical structure of discourse, appears as a way of trespassing or overcoming the fundamental solitude of each human being . . . that what is experienced*

> *by one person cannot be transferred whole as such to someone else. My experience cannot directly become your experience . . . Yet, nevertheless, something passes from me to you.*

Ricoeur does not express himself so very differently from Carl Rogers with regard to closeness. However, contrary to Rogers, Ricoeur does not reject the oppositional 'thrust towards explanation'. Like Lacan, Ricoeur focuses on limitations with regard to 'hearing' the other. Critical hermeneutics involve thus a phenomenological attempt to gain insight into the other's experience as 'lived' by the other person by 'bracketing' or putting aside one's own interpretive frameworks.

Critical hermeneutics also involve standing intentionally at a distance, with the aim of objectifying both the speaker and the hearer and the narratives through which they communicate – verbally, non-verbally and/or in enacted ways – and to consider patterns and structures within the stories. This opposite stance involves stepping back and considering one's framings – with a view, as Schön proposed, to being open to 'breaking' them open again, through the 'transaction with the situation'.

These moments bear certain parallels to Stern's earlier mentioned kairos moment, which reflects a closeness or merging that 'cannot last forever'. Green (2008: 19) writes:

> *'Now' moments . . . are spontaneous occurrences in a relationship, which reveal each part to the other in an authentic way, resulting in a reconfiguration of each person's sense of the other . . . changes within this intersubjective domain effect alterations at the psychic level of self and object representations.*

It is a 'fleeting moment' when the therapist surrenders, so to speak, in order to truly be on the client's side. According to ancient Greeks, Kairos was the god of the 'fleeting moment'. The 'immeasurable' qualitative shifts that occur through attending kairos moments are, as Ricoeur suggests, accompanied by an explanatory commitment, where we step back and view what has happened with some sort of distance. Merleau-Ponty (1999) captures this when musing on the meaning of a dialogue:

> *It is only retrospectively, when I have withdrawn from the dialogue and I am recalling it that I am able to reintegrate it into my life and make of it an episode in my private history, and the other recedes into his absence . . . Once the other is posited, once the other's gaze fixed upon me has, by inserting me into his field, stripped me of part of my being, it will readily be understood that I can recover it only by establishing relations with him, by bringing about his clear recognition of me, and that my freedom requires the same freedom for others.*

What has been referred to here in terms of a narrative commitment is difficult to put into words without becoming 'scientific' in the sense that Lyotard (1986) critiqued Habermas for submitting to the metanarrative of a technologically saturated modernity.

WHAT ABOUT EVIDENCE-BASED PRACTICE?

Evidence-based practice, with its scientific, objectifying language and structure, is often regarded as oppositional to reflective practice (see Knott and Scragg, 2008). However, the approach taken here implies a focus on Schön's dialectical thinking. Like critical hermeneutics, Schön's theory on reflective practice can be nourished by many types of inquiry. The idea behind this kind of dialectical thinking is that opposite framings can be beneficial; they can inform each other and reach new developments that remaining within one framing would prevent.

In the light of the emphasis paid today on evidence-based practice in counselling and psychotherapy, it is worth looking into other areas of mental health where evidence-based practice already has a firm foothold. Psychiatrists such as Ghaemi (2007) and Greenberg et al. (2003) adhere to the idea of a dialectic approach to psychological processes, as proposed by Karl Jasper, also inspired by critical hermeneutic and dialectical thinking. Ghaemi (2007: 181) argues for a combination of *Erklärung* and *Verstehen*, i.e. 'empirical observation and meaningful understanding'. Greenberg et al. (2003: 13) write:

> *In contrast to emphatic 'understanding', 'causal explanation' is stated in scientific terms and is believed to follow general laws like those characterising the natural sciences. It deals with factors, generally biological ones, operating at an extra-conscious level that can be studied using experimental methods . . . [However, when] we attempt to build up a picture of how someone's problems have evolved [we pay] attention to their previous experiences, their vulnerabilities and resources and their current life circumstances. These features are particular to the individual and . . . cannot be expressed in terms of general laws.*

Ghaemi (2007) suggests that our attempts to assess and categorise psychological and psychiatric diagnoses 'have gone too far'. There are 'too many diagnoses', and 'diagnosing has become hypercategorical'.

It is important to bear in mind, argues Ghaemi, that 'the diagnoses in DSM/IV are not "real" entities; they are abstractions'. (The *Diagnostic and Statistical Manual of Mental Disorders* (DSM/IV) has been developed by the American Psychiatric Association to provide standard criteria for classifying mental disorders.) No single patient exactly meets the specific criteria of any diagnoses; every patient is uniquely different in some way. Greenberg et al.

(2003: 13–14) also emphasise the importance of both understanding and explaining:

> *The assessment . . . heeds both understanding which is underpinned by 'reason' [and] empathic understanding and explanation, underpinned by causes. Both are necessary for a full account of the development of an individual's illness.*

Categorical knowledge, stresses Ghaemi (2007: 185), 'involves all-or-nothing qualitative phenomena – that is, something either belongs to category x or category y'.

ACTIVITY 4.2

An example of an assessment or a diagnosis based on categorical knowledge is whether or not someone is, for example, X = pregnant or Y = not pregnant. Ghaemi suggests that diagnosing instruments within mental health too often refer to symptoms as 'categorical knowledge'.

- Can you think of any presented problem in your practice that could be considered in the light of categorical knowledge?

MULTIDISCIPLINARY THEMES

The term 'illness' may sound alien to counsellors and psychotherapists. In fact, as suggested by Ghaemi's critique of present assessment and diagnosing tools, this is an area that is being reopened in psychiatry as well. As suggested before with the reference to Berg and a 'fourth wave' within development theory, there is a distinct multidisciplinary theme in our approach to the inner world of human beings today. Psychiatry, sociology, anthropology and psychotherapy are examples of earlier conflicting framing that now appear to overlap or learn from each other.

We have already mentioned integrative themes in the field of neuro-psychoanalysis. Green (2008: 1–2) from the Anna Freud Centre concludes that recent neurobiological findings 'leaves a window for biology to be surprised by some of the findings in psychoanalysis' – and presumably vice versa. Green continues:

> *Emotional life, the very stuff of psychoanalysis, is now gaining prominence as a focus for legitimate scientific interest . . . no single methodology alone does justice to the complexities of the human mind . . . The gap is diminishing and at the very least, the work of integration is on the agenda.*

Ghaemi also refers to recent neuroscientific discoveries as important steps towards the kind of dialectic approach we have talked about with regard to *Verstehen* and *Erklärung*. Allan Schore is a leading figure in this development. Schore (2008: 23) introduces the concept of neuropsychoanalysis:

> *Recent [integrative] models view . . . influences from the social environment as imprinted into the biological structures that are maturing during the early brain growth spurt, and therefore have long-enduring psychological effect . . . In a recent neuropsychoanalytic contribution I contend that . . . the structural maturation of the right brain is directly influenced by the attachment-relationship.*

REFLECTION POINT

Schore's neuropsychoanalytic approach (2008: 28) shows that the infant develops 'coping capacities to interact with the social environment' with the 'mother's [carer's] face as the primary source of visuo-affective information'.

Schore agrees that the importance of early dyadic experiences of 'affect synchrony' has been advocated by object relations thinkers for decades – for instance, by Winnicott who coined the phrase that 'there are no babies, only mothers and babies'.

Neurosciences make it possible to 'evidence' a process that object relation therapists have highlighted for decades – namely, that the original bonding between an infant and their care givers affects the child's development.

- Compare the evidence in neuroscience with the findings in traditional psychotherapy. How do you define 'evidence'?

DIFFERENT TYPES OF REFLECTIONS

In her theory about reflective practice, Beverly Taylor (2006: 15) suggests that we think in terms of three 'useful types of reflections' for professionals involved with care and health:

> *[I[t simplifies the enormous task of thinking about reflection if we imagine that there are three main types of reflection useful for people in any kind of practice: technical, practical and emancipatory reflection.*

Taylor pursues Jürgen Habermas's (1973) idea of 'knowledge constitutive interests' to meet today's requirements of evidence-based practice. Decision making is a complex matter, requiring a repertoire of reflective skills.

Taylor's different types of reflection (Taylor, 2006) are as follows.

- *Technical reflection* is based on the scientific method and rational, deductive thinking, and will allow you to generate validated empirical knowledge through rigorous means so that you can be assured that work procedures are based on scientific reasoning.
- *Practical reflection* provides a systematic questioning process that encourages you to reflect deeply on role relationships, to locate their dynamics and habitual issues.
- *Emancipatory reflection* seeks to free you from taken-for-granted assumptions and oppressive forces that limit you and your practice. In other words, this type of reflection lets you see what subtle and not to subtle powerful forces and circumstances are holding you back from achieving your goals.

Taylor stresses that:

> *Systematic questioning is the basis of all reflective processes. No type of reflection is better than another; each has its own value for different purposes and each type can be used alone or in combination with the other types.*

This thinking resonates with our thinking on how the practitioner moves between understanding and an explaining: *Verstehen* and *Erklärung*. It can also be explored with reference to the double-loop learning model.

CHAPTER SUMMARY

- The concept of 'epistemology' captures basic, underpinning beliefs from which knowledge is generated and inferences are being made in our daily work.
- The question of therapy as science or art is explored with reference to integrative frameworks based on integration-in-practice and dialectic thinking.
- Reflective practice can involve a carefully considered balance between different frameworks. It involves a combined perspective on 'empathic, reflective understanding and professional expert-stance'. This stance is explored with reference to what Ricoeur refers to as a dialectic relationship between a 'narrative' and 'explanatory' commitment when interpreting clients in psychotherapy.
- Dialectical thinking is ultimately about moving between knowing 'about' and knowing 'together' with the client.

CONTINUED EXPLORATION

Dialectical thinking will be pursued and expanded upon in the next three chapters. In the following two chapters Dr Biljana van Rijn will expand on dialectical thinking in terms of combining qualitative and quantitative research in therapeutic practice. As the Head of Clinical Practice at the Metanoia Institute, Biljana offers both theoretical and practical guidance within different types of knowledge and reflection with new policy making in mind. CORE and other evaluative tools are being introduced and put into the context of legislation and development within the state-regulated narratives on therapeutic practice. Biljana introduces concepts such as evidence-based practice, outcome research and efficacy research. These references will prepare you for the final stage of this book, where you are expected to identify 'measurable' targets with regard to your own practice. In Chapter 7, Professor Simon du Plock shares his insight and knowledge about how to 'research' a problem. Again, a dialectic stance is taken. Simon illustrates what, in this chapter, has been described as closeness and distanciation with regard to a problem, both experienced and owned by himself but also explored 'objectively' with distance through systematic inquiry involving research, observation, interviewing and further reading.

SUGGESTED FURTHER READING

McLeod, J (2001) *Qualitative research in counselling and psychotherapy.* London and New Delhi: Sage.

This is a highly recommended, accessible text about practice-based research for counsellors and psychotherapists.

CHAPTER 5

Developments within reflective practice

Biljana van Rijn

CORE KNOWLEDGE

- This chapter and the one that follows expand on how different *types* of reflection can nourish our practice and how we can incorporate different modes of reflection into our daily practice.
- Dialectical thinking will be pursued in this chapter and the one which follows with reference to qualitative and quantitative thinking and research. Different types of knowledge and reflection are explored with new policy making in mind. CORE and other evaluative tools will be introduced and put into the context of new legislation and recent developments within state-regulated narratives on therapeutic practice. The NICE guidelines will be explained and put into context.
- Key concepts such as evidence-based practice, outcome and efficacy research are introduced. These references will prepare you for the final stage of this book, where you are expected to identify 'measurable' targets with regard to your own practice.

INTRODUCTION

The emphasis on reflective practice since Schön has influenced psychotherapy and counselling, among other professions. Practitioners adopting this stance look at the therapeutic engagement as a narrative and assume that they are part of the process that unfolds between themselves and their clients. Both the therapist and the client bring their own subjective experience and cultural contexts into the room.

My own interest in this field stems from my personal experience, which I have integrated into my clinical practice.

BILJANA'S STORY

I moved to the UK from Yugoslavia in the 1980s. As in many such moves, this necessitated reflection on my personal and cultural identity. The civil war in the 1990s saw the disintegration of Yugoslavia as a political entity and I was faced with having to reflect on what this meant for me. I realised that every experience was subject to change, including certainties that most of us take for granted.

Reflection has helped me to become aware of my own narratives about culture, identity and my own history. As the new political regimes started to obliterate recent history (even the names of cities from my childhood changed), I realised that my own experiences and memories, reflected by my family and friends, had survived the changes.

These jointly created narratives offered a sense of security and rootedness. I was raised in the cultural and political context of Yugoslavia, with its particular mix of people, experiences and languages, and still think of it as my country of origin, although it is not a recognisable political label any longer. My life in Britain gradually became another part of my cultural identity, and this integration informs the 'cultural lens' through which I view the world.

As a psychotherapist I use this awareness of ongoing change processes to facilitate my clients' exploration of their own narratives to help them make choices in their own lives. Most of all, I hold certainties and 'givens' lightly, realising that everything is coloured by personal experience and culture.

From this perspective, I see the therapeutic encounter as an opportunity to engage in a unique process of exploration in which both participants take part.

Within this highly subjective enterprise, questions arise about how we generate professional knowledge to both enhance our practice and develop the profession as a whole.

Action research could provide an answer to this question. It is a broad methodology, which uses principles of reflective practice and provides a framework that can encompass different theoretical approaches and overcome the barriers between research and clinical practice.

In this chapter we will start by looking at different types of knowledge within reflective practice and then focus on action science and co-operative inquiry as methodologies that can be used to develop clinical practice.

KNOWLEDGE WITHIN REFLECTIVE PRACTICE

Hoshmand and Polkinghorne (1992) suggest that the focus in psychotherapy and counselling training needs to be the development of reflective judgement. Practitioners need to be able to use different sources of knowledge to develop their practice, and this includes scientific or research knowledge as well as knowledge emerging from clinical practice.

ACTIVITY 5.1

You need to do this exercise in pairs.

Take turns to tell the other a story about your first day at school:

- first, from a factual perspective;
- then from your perspective as a child;
- and finally from the perspective of your parent or carer.

What are the differences in your stories, and what are the similarities? Construct a narrative using the view from all perspectives.

Example:

The factual story I went to school when I was five. I was taken by my mother. I left my mother at the gate; she was crying. The teacher took me in and I joined a class. I met many children that day.

The child's story I was very excited about going to school. All my friends had already gone and I couldn't wait to join them. I was a bit lonely at home. My mum gave me a new dress; we bought it specially – it was yellow and had a little cardigan. I really liked it. It was warm and the sun was shining. The teacher took me in and I met all the other children. I saw my mother crying at the gate. I think she is sad about my father. She cries a lot. I felt worried, but then I went in with the teacher.

The mother's story Since my husband died last year I have spent a lot of time looking after my little girl. She is a great comfort for me. Today is her first day at school. I am proud and sad. Sad, that her father won't see her and it really hurts to let her go.

The listener's story I hear that your father died when you were young and you were living with your mother. She was grieving at the time you went to school. You were excited about going to school and being with other children. It sounded like it was quite lonely and sad at home.

Notice differences and similarities in these accounts. What have you gained from hearing all of them? How can you apply this to clinical practice?

With parallels to Beverly Taylor (2006) mentioned in Chapter 4, Park (2001) refers to different types of knowledge:

- *Representational knowledge, a functional type.* This type of knowledge is usually generated in more traditional research settings. Counselling and psychotherapy have benefited from advances in neuroscience and developmental psychology. For example, neuroscience has helped us to understand processes involved in dealing with trauma (Cozolino, 2002). Developmental psychology and experiments on attachment have helped us to understand the impact of early relationships on the human psyche (Bowlby, 1969).
- *Representational knowledge, an interpretive subtype.* This form of knowledge focuses on developing the understanding of meaning. The researcher (the 'knower') is assumed to come to this process as a whole human being, with history and personal traits, which impact on the process of knowing. For example, the practitioner may use their own experience of understanding what it is like to be a client to help them empathise with the anxiety their client experiences in the first session.
- *Relational knowledge, a relational subtype.* This type of knowledge focuses on the role of human relationships. It derived from each partner in the relationship and 'stays with both to become part of them' (Park, 2001: 85). This type of knowledge resides in the act of relating and shows itself in words, expressions and actions within the relationship.
- *Reflective knowledge.* This derives from the critical theory tradition – meaningful human knowledge must not only understand the world but also change it. This requires conscious reflection in change producing activity. Action is an integral part of reflective knowledge.

Case study 5.1 Mary

Mary is a woman in her 30s. She is a single mother who lives with her eight-year-old daughter. She works full time. Mary values her strength and independence. She has dealt with a number of difficult events in life by 'getting on with things'. She has a good social network.

While she was driving to work one day, her car was involved in an accident. It was a sunny day, and she was enjoying the drive and thinking about her daughter. Another driver suddenly pulled out from the slip road on to the motorway and the subsequent collision involved several cars. Mary remembered thinking that she was going to die. Her car tumbled and she heard a crashing noise and screeching. Then everything stopped. When she came to, she was in an ambulance. Later on, she found out that her car was completely smashed up and unusable. She had cuts and bruises but returned to work a fortnight later. Everyone was very pleased that she was alive, but then stopped mentioning it. Within a couple of weeks she became unable to go to work. She experienced panic attacks when she tried to drive, felt scared of going out or opening the door to strangers, and she was unable to go to the supermarket. She had nightmares about the accident and felt irritable and tearful.

ACTIVITY 5.2

What types of knowledge would you bring to understanding the client in the case study?

- *Scientific knowledge*. To understand her issues, it may be helpful to look up research on the impact of trauma. Is it possible that her panic attacks and nightmares are in fact flashbacks? Could she be suffering from post-traumatic stress? Explore what your theoretical orientation says about trauma.
- *Representational knowledge interpretive type*. Do you drive? Have you ever had an accident? What would you bring to working with Mary? Imagine yourself in Mary's shoes.
- *Relational knowledge*. How are you impacted by hearing her story? Pay attention to your sensations, feelings, images and thoughts.
- *Reflective knowledge*. Combine all these different sources of understanding. How would you approach working with Mary? Create a strategy.

ACTION SCIENCE

Action science (Argyris at al., 1985) was developed as an inquiry into social practice with the aim of producing knowledge in the service of practice. Practical problem solving within action science needs to be integrated with theory building and change. This is how action science aims to close the gap between research and practice. For a practitioner, this is related to the double-loop learning, explored in previous chapters.

For example, in order to address an issue that arises in the session, practitioners need to be aware of the narrative that they and the client are building and their own underlying theories of action. By evaluating these theories they are further developing their understanding and their theories of action.

As a research enquiry, the key features of action science, according to Friedman (2001), are:

- creating communities of inquiry within communities of practice;
- building 'theories in practice';
- combining interpretation with rigorous testing;
- creating alternatives to the status quo.

These are described in the following sections.

Creating communities of inquiry within communities of practice

Each practitioner using action science methodology becomes a researcher, building and testing theories of practice through their engagement with a client. By doing this, practitioners conduct research in practice, as opposed to the research conducted by professional researchers in laboratory settings.

Action science aims to help practitioners to discover the tacit choices they have made about their perceptions of reality, goals and strategies.

Case study 5.2

Sue is counselling Jane, who is talking about her relationship with her boss and his 'inappropriate attention' to her. Jane feels anxious about this. He often praises her work, smiles when he sees her and occasionally sits next to her when they have a break. She wants to know why he does this. Sue facilitates her, and they spend a session talking about his behaviour and motives. Reflecting on this session, Sue identifies that she felt anxious in the session. She identified the explicit aim of exploring the boss's behaviour and motives and an implicit aim, borne out of her own anxiety, to please Jane. She recognises that the impact of this was that they spent the session not focusing on the client, Jane, and her anxiety.

ACTIVITY 5.3

Reflecting on a session

You can use this exercise to reflect on a session with your client in supervision, or to practise in a peer group.

If you are in a peer group, organise a counselling session in a triad. Take turns to act as a counsellor, a client and an observer. Record your session.

If you are on your own, you can use this exercise to reflect on a recent session with a client.

Spend some time reflecting on your experience in the session:

- What did you think and feel?
- What was your sensory experience in the session?

Note down your reflections, and use them to formulate what you think was the main theme in the session.

Identify your explicit and implicit aims and the rationale for them.

What were your strategies as a counsellor?

Building 'theories in practice'

Human beings construct theories of reality that they continuously test through action. The objective of action science is to make those choices explicit. Action science aims to help practitioners to infer theories of action from observed behaviours so they can be critically examined and changed.

Case study 5.3

Sue felt uncomfortable after her last session with Jane. She reserved some time to consider why she and Jane ended up talking about Jane's boss rather than about Jane, the actual client. Sue identified the main theme as avoidance, based on the fact that the focus had shifted from the client to her boss. Reflecting on her interactions with her client, Sue realised that her anxiety and fear of being seen as 'inappropriate' if she misjudged the level of distance between her and the client in some ways mirrored the relationship the client had with her boss. She also recognised her own fear of being criticised, which related to her own upbringing. She used the transactional analysis concept of 'psychological games' (Berne, 1964; Hargaden and Sills, 2002), which describes the interlocking of unconscious relationship blueprints in the current reality, in order to identify the dynamic and the possible outcome of this process. On the basis of this, she identified that she needed to move out of this unconscious repetition and find a way of focusing on her client.

COMMENT

Return to your group reflection in Activity 5.3.

- Which theoretical concept would you use to describe the main theme of the session?
- What is your rationale for choosing that particular concept?
- Think of your interactions with the client and reflect on this part of your experience.
- Which theoretical concept would you use to understand this interaction and why?

Is there anything you'd like to change about it?

Combining interpretation with rigorous testing

In order to validate our understanding it is important that our personal interpretations are transparent and tested intersubjectively.

Case study 5.4

Sue shared this experience in her supervision group. Each of her peers responded differently to her presentation of the client. Mark fed back his experience of irritation about the client's interpretation of events. Magda empathised with the client's sense of hopelessness. Each of them recognised how their personal history impacted on their interpretation of the session. Sue became aware that her client's interpretation of the behaviour of her boss, as well as her own acceptance of it, were rooted in their individual experiences. This led to her to wonder what they might have missed in focusing on her boss's motives.

ACTIVITY 5.4

Consider the dynamics in Sue's supervision group, in Case study 5.4. Return to your own group from Activity 5.3. What are your similarities and differences, with regard to your outlook, theory and ways of working? Please explore and reflect with your joint session in mind.

- Ask your peers to share their thoughts and experiences. What are the similarities and differences between you?
- Reflect on your own reasoning. What part of your personal experience and history is affecting your interpretation of what happened?

Creating alternatives to the status quo

The aim of action science is not to facilitate knowledge per se, but to facilitate change for the benefit of the client and the wider community.

Case study 5.5

Sue explored the session from different angles: her own and her peers' subjective experiences; interaction with the client; and theoretical concepts she used. She decided in the next session to feed back to the client that she realised that in thinking about her boss's behaviour and motives, they had missed exploring what went on for Jane. She wanted to ask Jane about how she felt about the session to change the focus back to her client.

ACTIVITY 5.5

Reserve some time to consider your own group work from Activity 5.3 and compare it with how Sue has processed her session with Jane. How does your strategy differ and how does it overlap with Sue's? How do you normally develop a strategy? Does your strategy usually involve the stages referred to here, or do you assess and resolve work differently?

CO-OPERATIVE INQUIRY

Co-operative inquiry is a development within action research that focuses on addressing the power differential between a researcher (practitioner) and a participant (client). It concerns itself with the ethical issues regarding the ownership of the process. Who defines what happened?

Heron and Reason (2001) define co-operative inquiry as a way of working with other people to develop an understanding of one's own life and develop creative ways of looking at things as well as learning how to create changes. We can use this approach in clinical practice to understand that the therapist and the client are impacted by the therapeutic process and changed by it.

These are some of the characteristics of co-operative inquiry.

- All active subjects are fully involved as co-researchers. All participants take part in reflection and conclusions drawn from the process. If we look at therapy in this way, both the therapist and the client are involved in developing meaning within the sessions
- Co-operative inquiry involves an interplay between reflection, experience and action. In clinical practice both the therapist and the client are involved in reflection about the process. The practitioner might use a reflective diary, reflection in supervision, personal therapy and overt review sessions with a client. For the client this could also involve a personal diary and review session. Questionnaires could also form a part of this reflection.
- The experience involves action and changes in the outside world. This may be particularly relevant for the client. However, the therapist could also apply the learning from each client to their practice and their own life.
- The cycles of reflection, experience and action are repeated several times. The knowledge developed within this process can take different forms – words, concepts, expressions – and diverse skills – intrapsychic, interpersonal, etc. In clinical practice this means that both the therapist and the client will be reflecting on all of their experiential knowledge and using a full range of their human capacities.
- This type of inquiry can be informative (undertaken for the purpose of developing knowledge), or transformative. Transformative inquiry is particularly related to clinical practice and means that both the therapist and the client will to some extent be changed by their encounter.

Reflecting on this, we can ask ourselves whether knowledge developed in this way is valid.

Validity in co-operative inquiry

The notion of validity is one of the key concepts in research and the development of wider professional knowledge. However, the concept of validity in such an experiential inquiry is different from that of the traditional positivist research. Validity in this context depends on the ability of the participants to be reflexive and transparent about their knowledge. We do not aim to find absolute truths but to engage in ongoing cycles of inquiry and change.

The concept of mentalisation as an ability to think explicitly about the states of mind developed by Fonagy (Fonagy et al., 2002) refers to this type of thinking. In psychotherapy and counselling we can use theoretical concepts to help with this type of reflection.

One of the methods that can be used to develop the depth of reflection and open up the richness of personal experience is interpersonal process recall, or IPR (Kagan, 1967). This method involves live recollection of any interpersonal process and enquires into the subjective experience of each participant. The reflection is facilitated by a set of questions that serve as prompts in recalling the experience and deepening the reflection. Some examples of the questions that can be used to help the client and the therapist to recall the session are given in the research summary box on interpersonal process recall.

Research summary

Interpersonal process recall – inquirer's prompts

The purpose of these questions is to give clients and therapists space to explore the feelings and thoughts they were experiencing at the time of the original interaction. There are two roles:

- recaller – the person who is remembering the session – could be a therapist or a client; the recaller is in charge of the overall process;
- inquirer – the person who is using the questions to facilitate the recollection – the role of the inquirer is not to interpret or judge anything the recaller is saying.

Questions

1 Self-exploration
What thoughts and feelings did you have at the time?
Do you recall any physical sensations?

2. View of others
Did you have any feelings towards the other person?
What do you think they thought about you?

3. Own behaviour
Anything you were not saying?
Anything got in the way of how you wanted to be?

4. Values and assumptions
   Anything you liked about what was happening?
   Was anything taken for granted?

5. Social and physical environment
   Did the setting affect you in any way?

6. Hopes and intentions
   What did you hope to achieve, communicate?
   How did you want the others to see/feel towards you?
   Anything you would like to have said/done but felt unable to?

7. Past experience
   Has this happened to you before?
   Did the other's physical appearance/posture have any effect on you?

8. Reflection
   Any idea how you came to do that?
   Can you make any sense of that?

9. Closure
   Anything else?

Example

Recaller (client): I remember sitting at the chair, thinking, 'I don't know what to talk about.' I was thinking about my week. Remembering bits and pieces.

Inquirer: Do you remember any feelings or sensations?

Recaller (client): Slightly nervous, a bit too warm, sweating a bit. Then I said I wanted to talk about what happened at work that week. I remember looking at Mark (the therapist); he seemed a bit tense, but he had a sort of kind look in his eyes. I liked him. He seemed relieved when I said I wanted to talk about work, and I thought to myself that's OK then.

Inquirer: Was there anything you were not saying?

Recaller (client): I wanted to make it OK for him. He seems very young and I sort of didn't want to upset him, bring anything too complicated. I don't know him that well. I didn't want to be too much . . .

ACTIVITY 5.6

This exercise can be done in a triad with your peers. You can take turns to act as client, counsellor and observer.

- Client and counsellor engage in a practice session. The session is recorded. For the purpose of the IPR, once the session is finished both the counsellor and the client take the role of recaller. The observer becomes the inquirer.
- The inquirer plays the recording to the recaller (client). The recaller focuses on any memories of the session, aided by the recording, and recalls the session. The inquirer uses the questions to help the recaller remember the session.

Take turns so that both the counsellor and the client have an opportunity to explore their experience. The role of the inquirer is simply to facilitate and prompt, not to provide interpretations.

Take 30 minutes each to recall the session and then discuss this experience as a group.

As a group, discuss and agree what happened, and choose theoretical concepts to help you to conceptualise what happened in the session.

Share what you learned from this experience with each other.

CHAPTER SUMMARY

There are multiple sources of knowledge we can use to enhance clinical practice. We can draw on the epistemology of action research to help us reflect on these different areas of experience and knowledge. Park (2001) separates them into:

- representational knowledge: functional type usually generated in traditional research;
- representational knowledge: interpretive type focused on developing the understanding of meaning and involving the person of the practitioner;
- relational knowledge, which resides in the act of relating and shows itself in words, expressions and actions within the relationship.
- reflective knowledge, which emphasises the role of knowledge in creating change.

Different approaches within action research can be used to develop our practice and help us to develop it by engaging in cycles of reflection, action and evaluation. Action science (Argyris et al., 1985) and co-operative inquiry (Heron and Reason, 2001) are two methodologies within action research that can be used in this way.

CHAPTER 6

Evaluating our practice

Biljana van Rijn

CORE KNOWLEDGE

We have already reflected on the importance of the cultural context for the practice of counselling and psychotherapy. National policies that govern our profession are a part of that cultural context.

- In this chapter the author will present a brief history of psychotherapy outcome research and its impact on national policies about the provision of counselling and psychotherapy.
- We will particularly focus on the evaluation of practice and look at ways that reflexivity in practice can go hand in hand with evaluation.

HISTORY OF PSYCHOTHERAPY OUTCOME RESEARCH

The development of counselling and psychotherapy approaches since the 1960s led to their increased use in the treatment of mental health conditions in funded care. This called for investigation into their effectiveness, alongside other health interventions. It was important to know whether psychotherapy was effective and if so, which patients and mental health conditions it treated successfully and how it compared with other treatments, or even no treatment. A whole range of theoretical approaches is available within the professional field, and this raised questions about the effectiveness of individual approaches.

Research questions and methodologies used in psychotherapy outcome research were rooted in the tradition of positivist science, using the medical model of 'illness' and intervention. The body of outcome research spans decades, and its development is characterised by distinctive stages.

Research summary

The different stages of outcome research

Nathan et al. (2000) and Drozd and Goldfried (1996) are among the writers who give an overview of the stages in psychotherapy outcome research. They list the following developments.

1950s and 1960s

The research studies of this period often described the treatments and presenting problems inadequately. They were not always followed up, and it was difficult to know how long the improvements lasted. In 1952 Eysenck (cited in Nathan et al., 2000) evaluated those studies and came to the conclusion that psychotherapy was not particularly effective as a treatment. Two-thirds of clients improved without a treatment within a couple of years, and there was an inverse correlation between psychotherapy and recovery. This was a damning outcome that challenged psychotherapy researchers to develop their methodology and led to the next stage of psychotherapy research.

1970s

Research in the 1970s was conducted primarily by behavioural researchers. The research methods were improved and demonstrated the enhanced efficacy of psychotherapy. However, there were still criticisms. The majority of clients in these studies were students, and this raised questions about whether the findings could be generalised to the client population. Researchers continued to focus on developing their methodology. Even though the research demonstrated positive outcomes of psychotherapy, it did not seem to serve the clinicians. They were developing their practice using different sources of knowledge that did not rely on or influence the body of psychotherapy research. This was the starting point for the gap that developed between research and practice, which is still affecting the professional field today.

1980s onwards

Outcome research continued to see significant advances in research methodology. Clinical trials and new statistical methods of evaluation were developed. One of them, statistical meta-analysis, enabled researchers to conduct large-scale research and compare different studies. To demonstrate the efficacy of treatments, researchers needed to define the interventions carefully and take out variations in how different therapists applied their approach. Treatment manuals were developed. Outcome research thus evaluated the efficacy of manualised treatments for client groups with specific diagnosable condition (such as depression, anxiety, etc). This closely mirrored research within the medical field and demonstrated a much improved efficacy for psychotherapies.

EFFICACY STUDIES

Although the evaluation of psychotherapy using efficacy studies has demonstrated the usefulness of psychotherapy as an intervention, it also started a debate about its relevance. Efficacy was measured within a highly controlled laboratory setting; clients were chosen for the study and diagnosed with a single diagnostic category. Treatments were conducted by highly trained and intensively supervised practitioners. This raised questions about whether efficacy was the same as effectiveness and transferable to clinical settings where practitioners did not use manualised treatments and dealt with complex issues across several diagnostic categories. The debate about this has sometimes been described as a question of rigour versus relevance.

Efficacy studies are often seen to represent 'rigour' and the studies using more naturalistic, or effectiveness approaches are seen to represent 'relevance'. A brief description of each follows, in terms of 'efficacy' and 'effectiveness' research.

EFFICACY RESEARCH

This type of research is based within the positivist philosophy of knowledge and therefore aims to achieve high degrees of objectivity. To do this, there is an attempt to define and control the variables within the treatment and to demonstrate the researcher's objectivity. The actual person who is the researcher or therapist is not seen as relevant in this context. The emphasis is on evaluating and measuring the impact of interventions (such as cognitive behavioural therapy). When clinical trials are conducted, patients are either treated (experimental group) or given an alternative (control group); they are assigned to the groups randomly, and in single blind trials, they do not know whether they are receiving the treatment or not. In order to measure the impact of interventions, therapists conduct manualised treatments and use prescribed interventions and strategies. To determine the scope of therapeutic impact the patients are diagnosed using recognised diagnostic manuals such as the *Diagnostic and Statistical Manual of Mental Disorders* and given treatment according to their diagnosis.

Clinical trials are designed in such a way that other researchers can repeat them.

EFFECTIVENESS RESEARCH

Effectiveness studies focus on researching whether treatments are beneficial across broad populations of clients in existing clinical settings. They aim to develop clinical relevance, and show features that emerge in clinical settings and services during their practice with their usual clients (Barkham and Hardy, 2001; Mellor-Clark et al., 2001). Clinicians are not specifically trained to use treatment manuals. They practise in their usual way, using all the skills at their disposal in order to meet the needs of their clients. Clinical circumstances dictate the choice of treatment and clients are not being specifically chosen for the research. Outcome aims and measures are broadly defined. The improvements are measured in terms of their quality of life and subjective well-being, as well as symptom reduction.

CRITIQUE OF BOTH APPROACHES

Although methodologically rigorous, efficacy studies lack clinical relevance. Psychotherapists in clinical practice settings do not normally use manuals, and clients are not representative of clinical settings. For example, clients who present with depression may have very different underlying issues and come from different socio-economic and educational contexts.

Effectiveness studies lack rigour in research terms and therefore cannot be relied on in the provision of treatment. It is unclear who the clients are and what constitutes the treatment they are offered. Because of their structure they are impossible to replicate and therefore cannot provide objectivity.

THE IMPACT OF OUTCOME RESEARCH ON THE DELIVERY OF TREATMENTS

The issues of practice evaluation affect national policies on the provision of treatments. Psychotherapy and counselling are used as mental health treatments, and as such they are seen to belong within the natural sciences. The *clinical trial design*, already used in the evaluation of medical treatments, has also been used to evaluate psychotherapy in the US, and now in the UK. Government bodies, such as the Department of Health in the UK, are responsible for treatments offered in statutory sectors, such as the National Health Service. In the UK, the NHS trusts have a responsibility for clinical governance. Clinical governance policy gives NHS trusts responsibility for clinical quality in all the provision. The benchmark for the quality of treatments provided by the NHS is that they need to be based on *evidence-based practice*, defined as a 'conscious, explicit and judicious use of current best evidence in making decisions about the care of individuals' (Sackett et al. cited in Margison et al., 2000). The research evidence used to develop clinical guidelines is graded, and clinical trials are seen to reach the highest levels of research quality.

A different type of evidence, seen as complementary to evidence-based practice is *practice-based evidence*. Practice-based evidence (Margison et al.,

2000) is a framework for data arising from evaluating the delivery of services, and is often linked to more naturalistic effectiveness studies. Professor Simon du Plock approaches practice-based evidence from other angles in Chapter 7 of this book.

CLINICAL GUIDELINES

Clinical guidelines are developed on the basis of research evidence and inform the national policy on the provision of services. An example of this is the policy of stepped care within the NHS (see Figure 6.1). The only theoretical approaches recommended by the clinical guidelines are those that can be based on the body of research evidence.

THE GAP BETWEEN RESEARCHER AND CLINICIANS

The theoretical approaches not based on the body of outcome research suffer within this system. Although meta-analytic studies such as Wampold (2001) report that there are no differences in the efficacy of different psychotherapies, the body of evidence for efficacy of non-cognitive behavioural therapies is limited (Cooper, 2008).

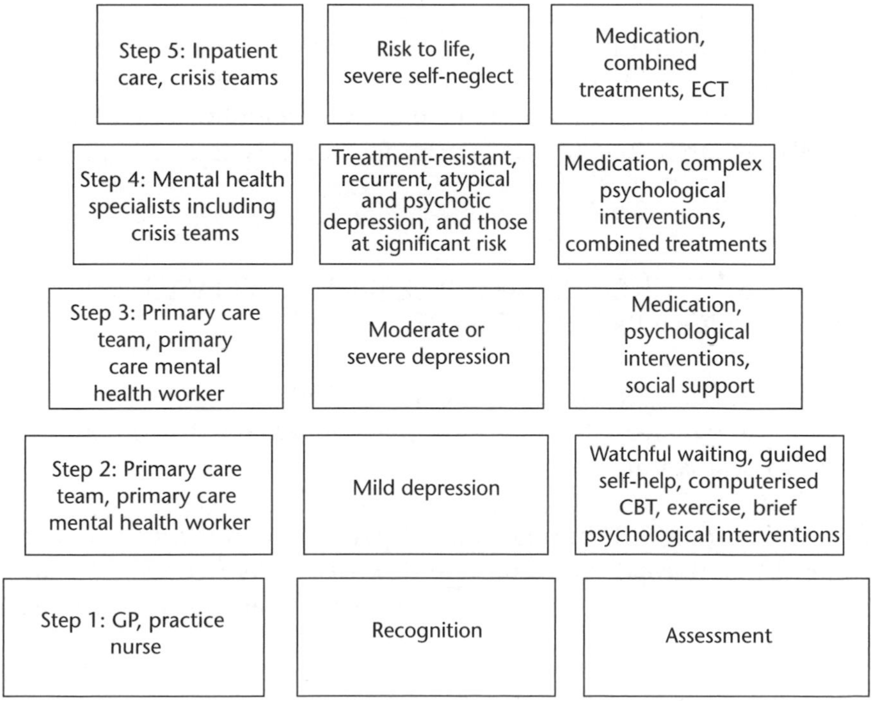

Figure 6.1: The stepped care model

Source: NICE (2007).

This demonstrates one of the wider impacts of the gap between researchers and clinicians on the breadth and provision of psychological treatments. Although to date clinicians have not significantly engaged in or impacted on research debates, this is starting to change. Counselling and psychotherapy courses are starting to put more emphasis on developing research skills and on the evaluation of practice, and clinicians in different organisational and practice settings are challenged to evaluate their own practice. This is expanded upon by Simon du Plock in the following chapter about practice-based research.

Professional umbrella bodies in the UK, such as BACP and the UK Council for Psychotherapy (UKCP), traditionally focused on clinical practice rather than research, but they are both now engaging in research debates and questions about clinically relevant psychotherapy/counselling research.

In order to move beyond the current divisions between different approaches to evaluation and address their weaknesses, there are efforts to integrate efficacy and effectiveness studies. Klein and Smith (cited in Nathan et al., 2000) suggest dedicated multi-site effectiveness/efficacy clinics. An example of this approach could be a highly structured, quantitative evaluation conducted in clinical settings, as currently developed within the NHS as a part of the efforts to improve access to psychological therapies.

Proponents of qualitative research, coming from the constructivist philosophical basis, argue that there is a need for a different type of evaluation. The needs of funding bodies could be met by developing a body of clinical case study research that focuses on in-depth analysis and evaluation of single cases.

HOW DOES PSYCHOTHERAPY RESEARCH AND EVALUATION AFFECT A SINGLE PRACTITIONER?

In this book we have been making a case for a reflexive approach to clinical work, aiming to increase the quality of practice. We see this aim as complementary to evaluation.

Within the current professional context psychotherapists and counsellors working in statutory, voluntary and independent organisations are expected to evaluate their practice, often using quantitative methods and questionnaires.

The author would like to suggest that evaluation of practice in general gives scope for professional accountability and aims to provide the best service for clients.

EVALUATING REFLECTIVELY

Evaluation is an important aspect of reflection-in-action (Schön, 1983) and allows a practitioner to recognise and reflect on their theories of action and make changes to their practice in order to meet clinical needs. Different methods of evaluation could help us to develop different forms of knowledge and add complexity to our understanding of clinical practice. In the previous chapter we discussed different sources and types of knowledge that can be used in clinical practice. They have complementary functions and can be used to develop a multi-faceted view of what goes on within a therapeutic setting. Our methods of evaluation need to mirror that process.

ACTION RESEARCH IN EVALUATION

One of the challenges in evaluating the process of psychotherapy and counselling is linked to finding the methodology that can help us to understand what really happened, and develop a rich and informative source of knowledge, helpful to the client as well as the practitioner. The action research structure of reflection, action and evaluation can provide a useful structure for this type of evaluation. It enables a practitioner to use both qualitative and qualitative methods and move beyond the science research gap.

Research summary

What methods can we use for evaluating our own practice?

Quantitative evaluation

This type of evaluation uses outcome questionnaires and measures. Practitioners are sometimes reluctant to use these methods for fear of adversely affecting the therapeutic relationship and anxiety about their own performance. However, research suggests that this type of evaluation offers clients an opportunity to give feedback to therapists. Sessional evaluation is shown to improve the therapeutic outcomes (Brown and Levinsohn, 1984; Miller at al., 2006). In the author's experience, clients can use evaluation as another way of taking ownership of the therapeutic process and engagement between the sessions. Therapists can use the evaluative measures as a tool for self-reflection.

Qualitative evaluation

The process of reflection-in-action can take place either within the session or after the session but during the treatment. The therapist can use different forms of knowledge and their subjective experience in order to reflect on the process, recognise their theories of action and change them to meet the requirements of their practice, as explored in previous chapters. It can be helpful to develop a structure for this type of reflection, for example, using recording and sessional transcripts, IPR, learning journal and clinical supervision.

The following case study is an example of how you might use different types of evaluation to reflect on your practice.

Case study 6.1 James and Christine

Christine came to counselling suffering from anxiety. She was entitled to a maximum of 12 sessions, paid for by her employer. She had been off sick for a month. Prior to this she had had a panic attack most mornings before going to work. While she was off sick, she did not experience panic attacks but had nightmares about work filled with anxiety. In the initial assessment James, the counsellor, asked her about work and she told him that there had been conflicts in her team at work for the last six months. She didn't want to 'take sides' and tried to have a good working relationship with both her manager and the colleagues. Both sides had become angry with her and started to shun her.

Using quantitative analysis for reflection

James has a practice of asking each client to complete a CORE Outcome Questionnaire (CORE Information Management Systems) at the beginning and the end of their work with him. Christine filled in the questionnaire, which showed that she presented above the clinical cut-off on all the different categories (Problems and Symptoms, Functioning and Subjective Well-Being) apart from Risk. Looking closely at the answers, James recognised Christine's high scores on anxiety, but also feelings of isolation and low self-esteem. These scores were congruent with what Christine had told him in the session, and he used them to enquire further into her experience. James used the scores for reflection and a qualitative inquiry. He asked further about her anxiety. Had she been anxious previously? How did she see the link between her work and feeling anxious?

Using phenomenological reflection

Willis (1999) refers to using phenomenology in reflective practice by using three modes of reflection.

- Practitioners are using *contextual reflection* when they uncover the social and cultural forces shaping the activity. In this case study, James is interested in the context and environment in which Christine is working. He discovers that her organisation is going through a major period of change, resulting in a very stressful working environment. He also recognises that Christine is the newest member of the team and scared of losing her job through redundancy.
- *Dispositional or self-reflection* refers to recognising one's own attitudes and beliefs. James has had an experience of being made redundant at work. Recognising this helps him to separate his own experiences from Christine.
- When using *experiential reflection*, practitioners contemplate practice as a lived experience by thinking back over what the event was like as an experience. James recognised that he felt swamped by the amount of detail Christine had given him in the session and wondered about what this meant. Did she feel she had to make sure she gave him the exact picture? Was she trying to make everything right? He was reminded of her trying to 'keep the peace' at work and decided to hold this as a possible theme for exploration. He used his theoretical background of transactional analysis to hypothesise that this might represent an unconscious historical pattern of pleasing others that his client was repeating.

COMMENT

All of these areas of reflection helped James to focus and identify what he thought were the areas for their work together. This is how, in the first session, James used the cycle of reflective inquiry – experience and reflection. This led to action, and together they devised goals for the session and some strategies. Their aims were to:

- help Christine to *reduce the level of anxiety by teaching her some skills* for relaxation and grounding;
- *reflect on the conflict at work* and help her to *develop a strategy* for dealing with conflict and her own feelings about the insecurity of her position;
- *recognise some of the underlying themes* in how she deals with conflict.

These aims were then evaluated during their work together and led to changes and adjustments. Another aspect of evaluation involved completing another CORE Outcome Measure (CORE Information Management Systems) at the end of their work together. James and Christine used the scoring to reflect on the questions and compare the two questionnaires. This gave Christine an opportunity to give feedback about her experience of counselling as well as reflect on the changes she made, and issues that stayed unresolved.

James works for an employer assistance agency, and the scores of his CORE evaluation will be used by the agency to evaluate his work and demonstrate the effectiveness of their service provision. In this way every single case evaluation can help to develop a body of practice-based evidence for counselling and psychotherapy work. For further information about CORE, please see the Appendix.

ACTIVITY 6.1

It is suggested here that clients can use evaluation as another way of taking ownership of the therapeutic process and engagement between the sessions.

- Consider to what extent evaluative measures involves Christine in the therapeutic process.

Therapists can use the evaluative measures as a tool for self-reflection.

- Consider the way in which James uses the cycle of reflective enquiry, i.e. how he moves between experience and reflection, to action. In what way do you think that James uses the evaluative measures as a tool for self-reflection?

CHAPTER SUMMARY

- The body of psychotherapy outcome research since the 1950s is characterised by distinct stages. They demonstrate the increased efficacy of psychotherapeutic treatments and the development of complex research designs. At the same time a gap between researchers and practitioners has been formed and it has increased over time.
- National policies affecting the provision of psychotherapy and counselling are based on the concept of 'evidence-based practice'. The research used as appropriate evidence for treatments is based on the medical model of illness and a positivist philosophy of research. There are current debates about different types of research that can be used to evaluate psychotherapy and counselling.
- Evaluation of practice, using action research methodologies, can help practitioners to evaluate their clinical practice in depth, using both qualitative and quantitative methods of inquiry.

CHAPTER 7

The vulnerable researcher

Harnessing reflexivity for practice-based qualitative inquiry

Professor Simon du Plock

CORE KNOWLEDGE

- This chapter brings us back to the subject of reflexivity and expands on what originally was referred to in terms of the essence of reflective practice as 'harnessing' the process towards transformative learning.
- Effectiveness research, which captures the ongoing process of therapeutic practice rather than measuring separate events, is further explored.
- Research can come across as 'frightening'. This chapter aims to demystify the process through references to a life-altering experience that is turned into practice-based research.
- The distinction between naive and systematic inquiry is explained and explored. Research involves moving 'from subjective experiences towards more general experience' via a 'helicopter view' – where you 'rise above the situation'.
- The concept of 'owning' one's problem is illustrated using a personal experience as an area subjected to systematic inquiry.
- This chapter brings another angle to what in Chapter 4 was referred to as a dialectical move between distanciation/*Erklärung* and closeness/*Verstehen*.

INTRODUCTION

We have paid attention, so far, to how reflexivity can enrich our clinical therapeutic work. I want now to encourage you to think about the contribution reflexivity can make to our research activities. In doing so, I want to go beyond 'talking the talk' towards 'walking the talk' – by which I mean that I will pursue my line of argument by providing an example of my own research. In doing so I hope to demonstrate the impact of this strategy on both the prime researcher (in this instance myself) and participants/co-researchers.

Therapists who take reflexivity seriously are ideally positioned to generate forms of research grounded in first-person experience and naive inquiry. I will outline the preliminary stages of such research to illustrate how this subjective experience and the specific research trajectory it entails provide a source of thick description and hypothesis that may be explored further with co-researchers.

RESEARCHING THE EXPERIENCE OF ILLNESS

The early stages of such an inquiry are not dissimilar to the process of reflection and analysis to be found in the practice of humanistic (and especially existential) therapy. The particular study I will use as my vehicle for discussing reflexivity in research suggests that diagnosis of a chronic illness may precipitate a profound shift in identity that can be exacerbated or engaged with creatively according to the differing relational styles adopted by healthcare professionals. I hope you will be able to see the ways in which being (or at least striving to become) an explicitly reflexive researcher provided me with insights and rich descriptive material that would not otherwise have surfaced. I include a number of exercises that I hope will prompt you in your own reflexive journey in relation to your sense of self as an inquirer/researcher.

DEMYSTIFYING THE NOTION OF 'RESEARCH'

I have argued (2004) that we therapists are in a fortunate position with regard to research. When we are confronted with research we are ourselves primarily researchers in our everyday activity as we go about our business of providing therapy. As McLeod (1994: 4) points out, we are constantly engaged in 'research' as we go through life and in our clinical work.

> *A counselling session with a client can be seen as a piece of research, a piecing together of information and understandings, followed by testing the validity of conclusions and actions based on shared knowing . . .*
> *A useful working definition of research is: a systematic process of critical inquiry leading to valid propositions and conclusions that are communicated to interested others.*

We get into difficulties, it seems to me, when we forget this and begin to see research as something different and separate from what we are already intimately involved in.

As an aid to reflection, I find it helpful to ask myself 'Where am I with research?' In prompting myself in this way I am making use of my existential-therapy training, and I am thinking of Rollo May's observation in *Existence* (1979) that where we are in terms of our relational world is often a more useful question than how we feel. So if I follow this guidance, I can ask myself 'Am I even in the room with research?' and 'What do I mean when I use the word anyway?'

INTIMIDATING CONCEPT

The word 'research' itself can feel intimidating: if you are not a graduate, then you may believe (erroneously, I think) that you are a stranger to research; if you have an arts degree, you may feel estranged from the sorts of 'scientific' research increasingly required in the therapy field. Perhaps worst of all, if you have a psychology degree, you may have found yourself working with statistical models and computer packages that seem to deliver little of direct relevance to your understanding of the human condition. I recall in my own psychology undergraduate degree that the emphasis was on the generation of statistically significant findings – and 'human being' was obscured beneath a concern with observable, measurable behaviour. There is nothing essentially wrong with this, of course, especially given that undergraduate psychology is not primarily concerned with therapy, but in the absence of careful reflection it is easy to invest research with past meanings and fail to see its present possibilities. One response to the anxiety to which the notion of research can give rise is to simply reject it as a valid enterprise – in the face of the 'otherness' of research we may defensively say it is 'not what we do'.

Research summary

If I am to take reflexivity seriously, I need to ask myself whether it is something that I do. In engaging with, rather than distancing myself from, research, I notice once more the relevance of a therapeutic approach to this question. It is interesting to recall the formulaic intervention 'I wonder what you mean when you say x?' While it is to be hoped that our interventions vary in tune with client material, this still seems to be a useful question and, like most useful questions, it is worthwhile asking it of ourselves. So if I ask myself 'When do I think I am doing research?', I find I respond with a large number of examples including the following.

- A trainee asks me whether I can suggest any literature on x, a topic for which they have been unable to locate any texts.
- I am invited to facilitate an 'away-day' for a group of clinical psychologists wanting to reassess their professional goals.

- I reflect (or self-analyse) on an aspect of a therapy session and refer to a paper on this aspect to help me explore further.
- I read about dementia after a relative has been diagnosed with the condition.
- I take an issue from therapeutic work to peer supervision.
- I am prompted by the lack of published material on similarities between existential therapy and cognitive-analytic therapy to write a paper that attempts to address this gap.

While, typically, only the last of these examples would be considered to constitute research as it is generally defined, I think that each provides an example of a form of research when this is considered more broadly and creatively. Each calls me into a particular engagement with the world, one that is characterised by an attempt to explore and make new connections between aspects of this world. Clearly these activities are distinct from the kind of carefully controlled laboratory-style experiments that are designed to fit the criteria of reliability, validity and generalisability (two, at least, might also be viewed as therapy or self-development). Nor are they similar to the observational studies, case studies or surveys and questionnaires that researchers often employ. Perhaps these activities might be termed 'inquiry' rather than research, as I am, in each instance, enquiring about my world.

In this regard, I am reminded of the model of the person as a problem-solving investigator of their world. In this sense I would want to argue that the sort of inquiry of which this chapter is a product should count as research.

ACTIVITY 7.1

This exercise is designed to help you begin thinking about the ways you use the notion of research, and the extent to which these are examples of 'accepted wisdom' or reflect the needs of your own personal and professional journey. You might undertake this exercise individually, or by working in pairs.

- If working individually, write down what comes to mind when you ask yourself the questions 'When do I do research?' and 'How do I know when I am doing research, and not some other activity?'
- If working in pairs, you might take turns to speak while your colleague scribes for you. When you have generated a response to these questions take some time to reflect on these, either individually or in dialogue. In particular, notice how you feel about your responses, and whether you would like these responses to be different in some regard.

RESEARCHING ILLNESS

Two significant life events – being diagnosed in late 2006 as having myalgic encephalomyelitis (ME/CFS) and the opportunity in 2007 to lead a research (as against a professional) doctorate – have encouraged me to think more deeply about the nature of inquiry. (I shall use 'inquiry' and 'research' interchangeably in this chapter.) Both these events have added substance to my assertion that the researcher's identity – their sense of who they are – is as crucial a factor in what they can illumine as it is in the practice of psychotherapy. The notion of the neutral, objective researcher is as absurd as the notion of the neutral, objective therapist. In both cases the illumination they can provide depends upon who they are – or perhaps where they are – in relation to either the client or the topic of research. I find it helpful to conceptualise this 'whereness' in terms of 'research trajectory', by which I mean the angle at which the researcher enters into an explorative process. The angle at which we enter any field of inquiry determines what is illuminated, and also what is thrown into shadow. I say 'thrown into shadow' because there is neither light nor shadow prior to the advent of the inquirer. As this trajectory serves to privilege some aspects of the phenomenon under consideration, and obscure others, it is important for us to be aware of our subjective stance at the outset of the research.

Rejecting the possibility of being a neutral investigator, I need to describe clearly my own research trajectory in relation to the experience of being diagnosed with a chronic illness. In some respects, I am attempting no more than to take seriously the axiom of existential-phenomenological investigation that the 'co-researcher', a term used to indicate the co-constructedness of 'reality' entailed in both therapy and research, should pay appropriate attention to the meanings they bring to the phenomenon under consideration.

REFLECTION POINT

Ruth Behar (1996: 13), writing about 'humanistic anthropology', makes clear that researchers who locate themselves in their own texts forfeit the defensive position of 'scientific observer':

> *Writing vulnerability takes as much skill, nuance, and willingness to follow through on all the ramifications of a complicated idea as does writing invulnerably and distantly. I would say it takes yet greater skill . . . To assert that one is a 'white middle-class woman' or a 'black gay man' or a 'working-class Latina' . . . is only interesting if one is able to draw deeper connections*

> *between one's personal experience and the subject under study. That doesn't require a full-length autobiography, but it does require a keen understanding of what aspects of the self are the most important filters through which one perceives the world and, more particularly, the topic being studied.*

I find Behar's words resonate very strongly with me, and it is for this reason that I have included the notion of 'the vulnerable researcher' in the title of this chapter.

ACTIVITY 7.2

What comes up for you when you read Behar's words? This exercise is designed to help you begin thinking about what you invest in research, and what it might be like for you to include yourself within your research in appropriate ways.

This exercise is best undertaken in pairs. Take turns to pose the following questions to each other:

- Who do I think I am when I say I am a researcher?
- What does this sense of self as a researcher include, and what does it exclude?
- What might it be like to expand what is included within this notion of researcher?
- What would be the advantages of expanding this notion?
- What do you think some of the costs might be?

When you have generated a response to these questions, take some time to reflect on these. In particular, notice how you feel about your responses, and whether you would like these responses to be different in some regard.

CHANGE OF PROFESSIONAL IDENTITY

The *raison d'être* of the Doctorate in Psychotherapy jointly offered by Metanoia Institute and Middlesex University is the promotion of research by fully qualified therapists that emerges out of their clinical and professional practice and that makes a distinct contribution to the scholarly community of therapists. My role in relation to the Doctorate has given me the chance to take forward ideas that I had expressed some years earlier (du Plock, 2004: 32):

> *We need to take more seriously the idea of research as a personal journey of discovery, or perhaps re-search, a continual transformation process*

rather than a discrete event. Research must not, of course, remain only of personal significance if it is to have any impact on professional practice – it must be disseminated, and evaluated by our peers, colleagues, and clients.

The researcher-practitioner is at the heart of this activity, since it is they who reflect on their work to identify what is needful, and they who at every stage of the research are required to engage with others in their specialist field to ensure the relevance of their work. This researcher-practitioner ethos is underlined by the requirement that their activities not only are conducted at doctoral level (i.e. can be mapped on to an agreed set of doctoral descriptors) but also generate a 'product' – a specific innovation in the form of a text, training programme, new research tool, etc. – that 'makes a difference' to clinical practice. This ethos is congruent with my own conceptualisation of the inquirer as the central, reflexive focus of the activity.

REFLECTION POINT

If we are to take this notion of the researcher's role to heart, we need to know about the journey they have taken to generate their product. An account of the research journey may provide information as significant as anything encapsulated in the formal outcome of the inquiry. It also evidences via thick description their research trajectory, and in doing so enhances the validity of the inquiry. It makes no more sense to think about objective inquiry as separate from the researcher than it does to think about the client isolated from the therapist – each co-constitutes the other.

CHANGE OF PERSONAL IDENTITY

The impact of the experience of illness on sense of self and identity has received considerable attention, particularly from the symbolic interactionist perspective (Bury, 1991; Charmaz, 1983; Corbin and Strauss, 1987). A number of writers have used their findings to explore the specific problems presented by chronic illness, including chronic fatigue syndrome (Clark and James, 2003). My diagnosis as having ME presented me with a radical challenge to my sense of identity in a number of ways, some of which are relevant here. Diagnosis typically entails an 'expert' of some kind making a judgement about another person who, generally, is considered a 'non-expert'. In medical terms a doctor tells their patient that they 'have' a certain illness or condition. When the patient is a psychologist and the condition one generally thought to be at least partly psychosomatic in nature, the authority and power in play become complex and problematic. This is perhaps particularly so given the existential-phenomenological critiques of diagnosis with which I became familiar in the course of my own therapy training. It may also be that my previous way of constructing a sense of self heightened the challenge of this diagnosis; as Aujoulat et al. (2007: 9) argue in their research into the experience of chronic illness:

> *People who had previously enjoyed being in control of things and who described themselves as having a managerial type of personality appeared in our study to be at greater risk of experiencing a feeling of loss of their sense of identity.*

I found myself thrown into a process of inquiry in which I was not merely the prime researcher but also the primary subject, as I sought to engage with questions such as 'How do I feel about "having" an illness?' 'How might ME impact on my sense of identity?' 'What does it mean to be a psychotherapist with a chronic debilitating condition?' As a psychologist I found it natural to reflect on this challenge by reading in depth about ME and keeping a diary to structure what at least initially seemed a situation over which I could exercise little control.

HELICOPTER VIEW

At the outset I did not specifically frame as research the literature search I undertook or the diary in which I recorded my subjective experience both of the condition and of my interaction with healthcare professionals. When I rose above the situation to take a helicopter view, I conceptualised them as subjective strategies adopted in response to a personal situation. In the case of diary-keeping, I was informed by my knowledge of the therapeutic effects of writing structured accounts of stressful experiences (Hunt, 2000; Hunt and Sampson, 2002; Pennebaker, 1993; Philips et al., 1999). I soon noted, though, that I found both activities therapeutically useful, and I began to make connections between this insight and my existing professional knowledge. As an example, I visited NHS and other websites on ME and chronic fatigue syndrome (CFS) after my diagnosis and felt reassured to discover how precisely the label mapped my symptoms, even though they invariably emphasised the limitations of the few available treatments. This reminded me how therapy clients often seek a label for their condition and can be dismayed rather than relieved when therapists cannot or will not provide one. Similarly, I found I kept increasingly detailed verbatim accounts of my meetings with healthcare professionals. Writing these records assisted me in de-briefing; it also helped me to obtain an enhanced sense of mastery, as I was able to identify their different relational styles.

FROM NAIVE TO SYSTEMATIC INQUIRY

This movement from subjective experience towards more general (I would not say objective) experience meant that soon my idiosyncratic questions were re-framed as:

- What does it mean to 'have' an illness?
- How might a diagnosis of ME impact upon sense of identity?
- What is it like for a psychotherapist to be diagnosed with a possibly psychosomatic condition?

I found relatively little had been written – or at least published – addressing these questions. This led me to further hypothesise the following:

- there is something about the identity of 'psychotherapist' that makes it difficult for us to engage with our own experience of illness.

In this connection I noted that Bayne in *The needs of counsellors and psychotherapists* (cited in Varma, 1997) writes about emotional self-care, though primarily in terms of using strategies to cope with stress.

Without necessarily doing so in full awareness, I found I had taken my diagnosis and actively sought to understand it as 'a continual transformation process' with which I developed a close relationship, rather than accepting it passively as a victim. I also found paradoxically that in closing with it to make it my own, my inquiry became one of more than just personal significance. In the wider inquiry that I undertook, and that I plan to write up for future publication, I found I journeyed from a descriptive self-analysis of the type with which phenomenological inquiry can open to a consideration of the co-constitution of relationship in the course of professional consultation.

MOVING FROM NAIVE INQUIRY TO RESEARCH

In the process above, I moved from naive inquiry – the acquiring of information which we do on a daily basis – towards research/inquiry. In distinguishing between naive inquiry and research, Barber (2006: 89) says:

> *to qualify as research, your inquiry must involve a careful searching, your method of collecting information must be located within a recognizable methodological tradition, and you must demonstrate systematic investigation and critical reflection upon both what you are doing and how you are doing it. You need also to illuminate your motivation and rationale and what influences you at the time.*

RECORDING REFLECTIVELY

The diary in which I recorded accounts of my meetings with each of the health professionals involved in my treatment provided a way of keeping track of this complex process, since five professionals played a role: two general practitioners, a practice nurse, a medical herbalist and a clinical psychologist. While my thinking was that maintaining a record would allow me to 'stay in the driving seat' in a pragmatic sense, I soon noticed that writing functioned as a way of de-briefing. I moved from recording primarily factual information to a more comprehensive reflection on my feelings prior to, during and following each meeting. I found that I looked forward to meetings with the clinical psychologist and medical herbalist, even though both entailed a fatiguing journey of several miles. In contrast, I generally felt apprehensive about my meetings with the GPs and practice nurse, even though the surgery was a short walk from my home. I also noticed that I wrote verbatim notes after visits to the GP surgery, while I often recorded only a summary of meetings with the psychologist and herbalist. This structured inquiry had clear therapeutic functions for me in helping me to make distress and confusion meaningful.

ACTIVITY 7.3

I agree with Sousa (2007) when he argues that therapy and research should not be conflated; I would also suggest that, while it is often important to conceptualise them as distinct activities, research can be therapeutic, and therapy involves exploration akin to research.

Reflect on the following in pairs:

- Think about ways in which you seek to engage with difficult or challenging events in your own life.

Do they share any similarities with the strategies I have described? Perhaps they are very different? To what extent do they enable you to generate new perspectives on and wisdom about an aspect of living? Do these ways of being relate in some ways to how you think about the world when you are being a researcher?

THE EMERGENCE OF AN ORGANISING THEME: 'OPENNESS TO RELATIONSHIP'

Within the first month of treatment the theme of 'relationship' surfaced to link my observations. As an existential-phenomenological therapist I am constantly aware of ways in which I can hold myself open to, or close down, the possibilities of being-with-the-client. I know that a number of factors are involved in this, including my willingness or otherwise to hold myself open for the experience that May et al. (1979) describe as the experience of 'here-is-a-new-person'. Our ability to encounter the other in this open manner is a prerequisite according to May for the other to have an 'I-am' experience. While I have sometimes become aware of the I-am experience as a therapy client I had not previously had this experience within a relatively short time of working as a client with five different healthcare professionals. I found it instructive and illuminating to reflect on the ways in which each embodied a relational style that to some extent determined their availability for relationship. These reflections became a major organising theme in my research diary. Typically (and I had numerous meetings with these five professionals), I found I felt less unwell after meetings with the herbalist and psychologist. The herbalist, medically trained but without a counselling background, tended to present as interested and available for encounter. Briefly, her focus was holistic (she would ask me open questions about myself, and discuss various options and recent research in a relatively equal way, free of jargon). She did not attempt to hide herself but, equally, did not disclose inappropriately. She presented smartly but relatively informally in terms of dress, and sat to the side of her desk while taking notes. I found it interesting and reassuring that she was transparent in this way, permitting me, for instance, to follow her train of thought when she was considering various prescriptions. Appointments were for 30 minutes but often extended to 40 minutes. Her boundaries were flexible but holding. My sense was that she was available but kept secure boundaries. Reflecting on this, I felt that her style of engagement was broadly similar to that to which I aspire in my own clinical work.

I found that my therapist, an experienced male clinical psychologist in his early or mid-forties, was generally open to a relationship based on mutual understanding. It was disarming, especially as an existential practitioner, to be greeted at our first appointment by 'I've Googled you, and I feel I know you already!' My response 'Well, I've done the same to see what you've published' left us in a curious position. I think our mutual agreement that we would need to start from scratch to think about what work we might undertake together was, in the event, helpful and supportive. Perhaps the most helpful aspect of our meetings was that he resonated with my frustration with the shortcomings of the general practitioners and supported my referral to a specialist clinic. I noticed that I looked forward to our meetings and did not need to use my diary to de-brief to the extent that I did after visiting the GP surgery.

In contrast, the female nurse there made little eye contact and was concerned to take blood samples as quickly and efficiently as possible. She disclosed nothing of herself or her training, and her mode of relationship was of the 'doing-to' type. Frustrated at our first meeting that I admitted a fear of needles, she responded, 'You're my second needle-phobic so far this morning – it's not my day!' Perhaps unsurprisingly I felt 'unseen' in these encounters, except insofar as I fitted the category of 'difficult patient'. The senior of the two general practitioners, a middle-aged man, stayed behind his desk most of the time and kept his eyes on a computer screen. His mode of relationship was to use the computer as intermediary. Having typed information into it, he would share the 'factual' information it generated. One of his most puzzling announcements was 'How would it strike you if I told you that you have a 20 per cent chance of a heart attack in the next ten years?' I found this style of relating to me as if I were an audience for medical technology alienating; not only did I not feel seen, I felt that I had somehow failed to appreciate appropriately the technology with which the doctor was clearly enamoured. His colleague, a younger man perhaps in his late thirties, took pains to demonstrate his willingness to treat me as an equal by maintaining constant eye contact. So relentless was this that I began to fantasise that he had taken a short course in advanced empathy techniques. He explained in some detail what was known about ME. He seemed to thus invite my compliance with a long-term anti-depressant drug prescription and was baffled and defensive about what to suggest beyond this when I indicated I was not willing to take this route. While he agreed to refer me to a specialist clinic, he did so with the caution 'A lot of people expect a cure but there isn't one.' As I had explicitly stated that I was seeking ways of managing a chronic condition, this seemed to indicate that, regardless of the amount of eye contact, once again I had not been seen but had been categorised as one among 'a lot of people'. Moreover, this category 'a lot of people' was clearly viewed as problematic.

ACTIVITY 7.4

My experience, while I frame it in the context of being 'seen' by the other, reflects the findings of studies that have focused on patients' sense of self-determination and power. Such studies indicate that the key features of an empowering patient–medical practitioner relationship include continuity, patient-centredness, mutual acknowledgement and relatedness (Chang et al., 2004; McWilliam et al., 1996; Paterson, 2001). McWilliam et al. (1996) found patients experienced empowerment in the process of telling their story if the healthcare professional is able to facilitate a mutual exploration of their situation and situatedness. In doing so they argue that patient and practitioner collaborate to add or create meaning to the patient's experience. In contrast, Paterson (2001) finds that where the healthcare professional discounts experiential knowledge and provides inadequate resources, particularly in terms of time and continuity, the patient is likely to feel disempowered.

- Try to recall something from your own life – a negative experience where you continue to have strong emotions works best in this context. Relate it to your colleague.
- As you do so, notice how you tell your story. Do you organise the material in such a way as to reinforce an existing perspective that frames you in a particular role?
- Can you begin to think about ways of telling the story that might re-frame the material and make it more meaningful? Does the extent to which you feel 'heard' by your colleague assist you in such a re-framing?

'RELATIONSHIP' RE-FRAMED IN THE CONTEXT OF THE INQUIRY

Up to this point my observations were focused on the extent to which each healthcare professional was able to be in a relationship with me, according to my sense as an existential-phenomenological therapist of what the phenomenon of relationship might mean. I had noted how I felt more or less ill according to the extent to which each was able to encounter me. My thinking was increasingly that there might be a link between the experience of being 'seen' and feeling ill. As Charon (2006: 65, 66) asserts:

> *The healing process begins when patients tell of symptoms or even fears of illness . . . These narratives, or pathographics as they are sometimes called, demonstrate how critical is the telling of pain and suffering, enabling patients to give voice to what they endure and to frame the illness so as to escape dominion by it. Without the narrative acts of telling and being heard, the patient cannot convey to anyone else – or to the self – what he or she is going through. More radically, and perhaps equally true, without these narrative acts, the patient cannot himself or herself grasp what the events of the illness mean.*

As the inquiry widened, a further cycle of research evolved – I began to think about these communication difficulties more systemically as it seemed to me that the various healthcare professionals were not able to hear each other. My impression was reinforced by the wording of the King's College Chronic Fatigue (CFS) Research and Treatment Unit website, where I found a cautionary note (2007: 3) for prospective patients:

> *The perpetual battle for validation that most sufferers of CFS are caught in is literally, physiologically exhausting, depressing and dispiriting. It affects the course of the illness. No other sufferer of chronic disease has to fight this bizarre battle to have the facts that they live with every day legitimized by a hostile authority. As long as CFS has to prove itself, that much longer will sufferers suffer. As therapists, our first and last*

> *concern is to take the suffering of clients seriously. All this involves is listening.*

While the message seems to be directed towards patients, it is obvious that such a 'battle for validation' is primarily one between the healthcare professionals themselves. As the website (2007: 1) expresses it:

> *Some GPs are sceptical about the existence or treatment of CFS/ME. If you are having problems getting a referral for these reasons, you could perhaps try another GP in your practice.*

The casual wording belies a serious problem: such a request will probably be interpreted as a challenge to the power structures of many GP practices. A healthy person might find making such a request daunting, and it is likely to exacerbate the symptoms experienced by an ME sufferer.

CONCLUSION

To summarise the journey I have taken, I have – however briefly and sketchily – suggested that reflexivity enables therapists to ground their research in subjective experience and naive inquiry with confidence. My own personal and professional experiences have led me to an enhanced awareness of the 'self' of the researcher at the core of a reflexive process. A wealth of thick description of a phenomenon surfaces when we attend to the researcher's individual journey into the field. The thick description obtained at this early stage in the research journey provides a resource for reflection on later stages of inquiry. My own experience of a diagnostic process was the catalyst for personal identity questions and therapeutic activities that led to more general inquiry and the emergence of an organising theme – in this particular instance, that of health professionals' openness to being in relationship with the patient. This, in turn, led me to hypothesise about their openness to be in relation with each other, and the implications of systemic communication patterns for the patient's sense of self. While it is not always the case that the researcher is prompted by direct personal experience to embark on their inquiry, the resulting study is impoverished and, I would argue, less valid and trustworthy if the self of the researcher is excluded from their research journey.

- Reflexivity enables therapists to ground their research in subjective experience and naive inquiry with confidence, which is likely to benefit the level of insight and reflection throughout the systematic inquiry.
- The practitioner's own personal and professional experiences can lead to enhanced awareness and insights of the 'self' at the core of a reflexive process.

- While it is not always the case that the researcher is prompted by direct personal experience to embark on their inquiry, the resulting study is impoverished and, arguably, less valid and trustworthy if the self of the researcher is excluded from their research journey.

CHAPTER 8

Working towards transformative learning

CORE KNOWLEDGE

The chapter is aimed at guiding you towards the completion of your own manifesto in reflective practice.

- This chapter looks at the idea of 'transformative' learning with an 'extended abstract' stance. This is a stage in the reflective process when the experience or situation is being re-examined, transformed or 'recycled' and made useful, rather than shunned or ignored.
- Reflective learning involves moving between concrete experience, feelings, reflective observation, abstract conceptualisation and active experimentation. It is explored with reference to Kolb's and Gibbs's reflective cycles and to systematic inquiry, work-based learning and transformative learning.
- You are encouraged to identify a problem that prevents your practice from moving forward. You are advised to revisit your own reflective writing and look for situations, themes and insights that will help you identify areas for improvement, whether on a personal, cultural or theoretical level. The double-loop learning model is offered as a tool to help you get the most out of your reflective practice.
- The ACT SMART model provides a checklist to assist you in devising a strategy for your problem solving. It is used in this chapter to label the basic steps in your reflective cycle as you move from recognising a problem to transforming it into practice.

TOWARDS TRANSFORMATIVE LEARNING

Transformative learning ultimately involves the ability to take a broad view of a problem, an 'extended abstract' stance where principles are transferred, related and compared with principles and ideas in other areas. Atherton (cited in Roffey-Barentsen and Malthouse, 2009) compares the first stage of reflective practice with knowing some parts of a car when it breaks down;

you *notice* something – perhaps a rattling or a disconcerting noise, which suggests a problem.

'Making sense' is the next step, where we work out where the problem lies in comparison to other parts of the vehicle.

'Making meaning' is the subsequent stage in reflective learning. More connections are made; more general links are explored. We explore the different parts of the car with an interest in 'what goes where' without yet being able to claim full comprehension.

'Working with meaning' is the stage when we gain enough knowledge to make connections in relation to the whole. In the previous chapter, Simon illustrated this stage of reflective learning with reference to his own problem of chronic fatigue. He moved from a sensation of always being tired to a place where he viewed the symptom in a new context based on systematic reading, interviewing and observation of others and himself. This can be described as a transformed level in relation to the original problem; Simon reaches this stage by temporarily disowning the symptom and adopting a view of scientific distance akin to what in Chapter 4 was explored in terms of Ricoeur's term 'distanciation'. Simon moves away from the problem, views with distance and dissects it as if under a microscope. He challenges his prior understanding of his symptoms and even criticises them as potentially psychosomatic before reaching a stage where he is equipped to understand his illness in the context of a wide repertoire of insights into both chronic fatigue syndrome and the care process in general. The problem – in Simon's case the chronic fatigue – may not go away; the 'pathology', to use Sedgwick's words, is not eliminated. But it has been transformed to a level where it is 'known and utilised'.

REFLECTION POINT

In reflective practice and inquiry, objectivity is turned on its head. Parker (2004: 138) writes:

> *Psychologists sometimes argue that only quantitative research is properly 'scientific'. [However this argument] can just as well be turned around to put the quantitative researcher on the spot . . . The old laboratory-experimental 'paradigm' of research in psychology was . . . 'pre-scientific' and the task that quantitative researcher now faces is how to account for the reflexive capacity of human beings, the meaningful nature of the data they produce . . .*

This stance is based on the view that people are not 'tidy' or static; meanings develop all the time. Barber (2006: 4) reminds us of this when he writes about research:

> *to capture the complexity of individuals and groups, researchers need to: be aware of the whole holistic field; appreciate 'what happens when it happens' and 'how' it happens; incorporate sensory perceptions and imaginative visions; engage with the situation if an experiential, humanistic, vibrant and authentic way; and account for macro scales of society and micro influences of the society.*

- Could you be a researcher? Does the research referred to in this book fit in with your general or previous views?

RESEARCHING YOUR PRACTICE

Research as we have described it so far involves returning to, lingering over and elaborating on a problem. It is a matter of systematically searching and re-searching a particular area of interest. By actually referring to a problem of his own, Simon brings Ricoeur's concept of 'closeness' alive. The dialectic relationship discussed in Chapter 4 involved approaching the research subject with an ethnographic attitude, which means studying something by first 'living it' – standing in 'its' shoes, just as we do when listening to our clients in order to gain an insider's perspective of the presented phenomenon. In Chapter 7 Simon suggested that:

> *[w]e need to take more seriously the idea of research as a personal journey of discovery, or perhaps re-search, a continual transformation process rather than a discrete event.*

He also wrote:

> *It makes no more sense to think about objective inquiry separate from the researcher, than it does to think about the client isolated from the therapist – each co-constitutes the other.*

Biljana referred to this thinking in terms of action research that goes beyond static explanations by outside experts and requires 'sampling' through an active moment-to-moment inquiry. Simon's work rests on the contention that work-based learning is the 'field of study' (Portwood, 2003: 78). Significant for work-based learning is that learning projects are undertaken in the work place and orientated towards your personal work situation and real life problems. The learning process involves teasing out themes and patterns as part of your transformative learning. This thinking can be illustrated by the themes in Kolb's experiential learning cycle (Kolb, cited in Portwood and Costley, 2000) where concrete experience moves to reflective observation, then on to active experimentation, and then back to a (transformed) concrete experience. Gibbs (1988) has added emotions into the cycle. Their combined thinking is illustrated in Figure 8.1.

ABOUT YOU

Simon highlights the importance of 'owning' the problem by actually referring to a problem of his own. He also raises the important point that research requires a 'helicopter view', which can be compared with Ricoeur's idea of 'distanciation'.

You are encouraged to approach your own inquiry with this dialectic in mind, balancing and co-ordinating an inside and an outside view of a problem. The balance can be viewed with reference to the cycle in Figure 8.1, and can help you achieve 'order' in your inquiry.

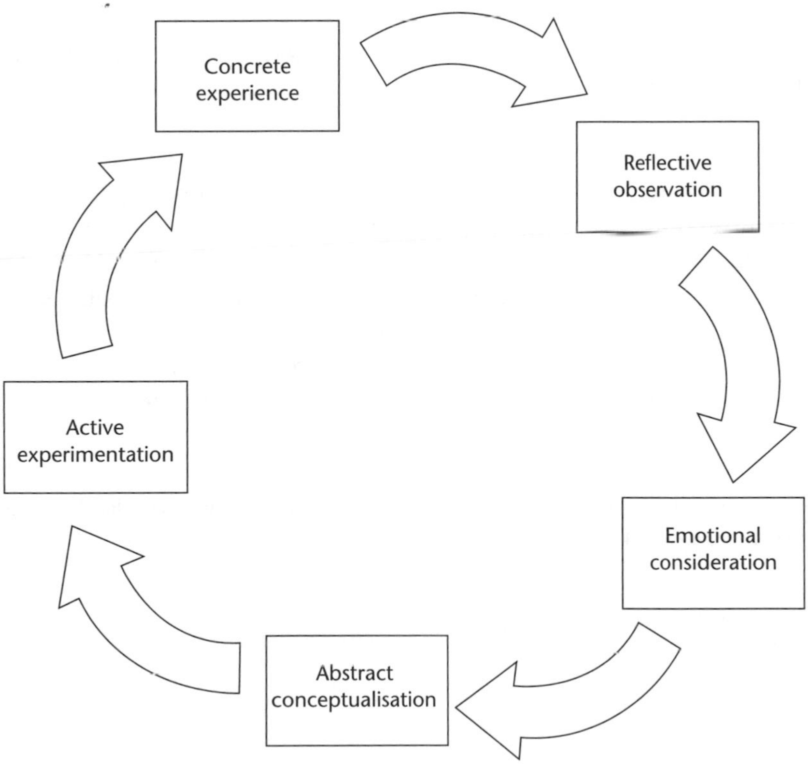

Figure 8.1: Reflective cycle based on Kolb's and Gibbs's thinking on the different stages of reflective learning

Research summary

Objectivity, validation and reliability?

The terms 'objectivity', 'validation' and 'reliability' are often used in research. The traditional, natural scientific meaning of objectivity assumes a neutral stance, with the researcher engaging with research as a 'sterile surgeon'. Validity implies that different ways of studying something should lead to the same conclusion. Validity in this sense is meant to guarantee that the actual research has not influenced the outcome. The term 'reliability' traditionally involves the requirement 'that the study remains stable over time rather than being liable to change' (Parker 2004: 137). The way research has been approached within this book is that research about people never can meet these requirements. Parker writes:

> *The nature of the material that is studied by a science needs to be understood. Qualitative research focuses on the way in which meaningful qualities of human 'experience' or 'subjectivity' are represented to others.*

Turning objectivity on it head is not the same as disregarding it. The importance of a systematic approach remains.

If we are to 'replace' or reconstruct the meaning of objectivity, validity and reliability, we need to think about the following requirements, as identified by Parker.

- Objectivity? Have you described what theoretical resources you use and rely on, to turn your subjectivity into a useful device? How can others understand and evaluate how your input has impacted on the research and its outcomes?
- Validity? Have you been clear about the ways in which your account is distinctive and pragmatically different from others?
- Reliability? Have you traced a process of change in your own and others' understanding of the problem? Have you explored how views of the problem or topic may continue to change?

Parker suggests that we think of the criteria for 'good' research with the following key concepts in mind. Research should be:

- grounded;
- coherent;
- accessible.

IDENTIFYING A 'PROBLEM'!

When you STOP, LOOK and LISTEN, what do you see? What you identify as a 'problem' and a topic for your reflective, systematic inquiry is for you to decide. It can be a matter of an already occurring problem or theme, but it could also revolve around issues that may cause problems at a later stage. It may concern ending therapy sessions, discussing fees or keeping your time boundaries? Or maybe you identified some other problems in Activity 2.4 about the 'rescuing trap'. Rereading your stories will probably highlight some themes or recurring issues. Some of you may find yourself caught between conflicting underpinning values, like Allan who wanted to save all marriages, or Liza whose underpinning religious beliefs clashed with her humanistic theoretical framework.

SINGLE- AND DOUBLE-LOOP LEARNING

Below is an example from the case study with Allan. As you may recall from Chapter 1, his problem surfaced in supervision. His explicit strategy involved a psychoanalytic thinking that addressed unconscious motives behind partner choice. Allan's espoused theory suggests that old fears and fantasies are reactivated in adult relationships and that to identify projective identification and other unconscious processes is something that Allan both believes in and is trained to work with. His expected outcome is, in other words, to bring unconscious motives into awareness. As you will see in Figure 8.2, the 'outcome' box is divided in half. One part indicates the expected outcome and the other refers to what actually happened. In Allan's case, premature endings was something of a pattern – he was consistently failing to 'keep' his clients.

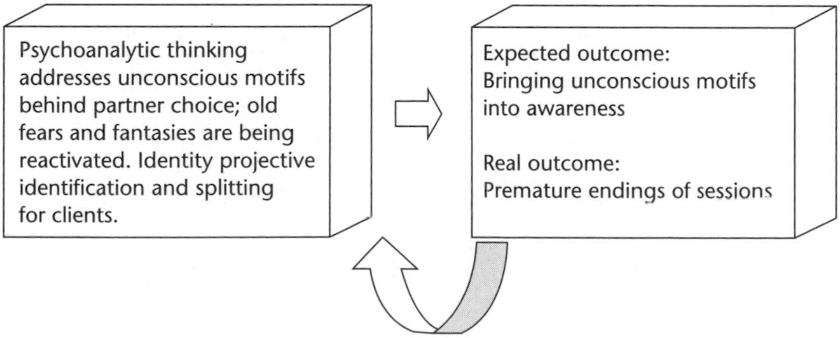

Figure 8.2: Outcomes: single-loop learning

Consider a scenario where your expected outcome differs from what actually happens. You may choose the model in Figure 8.2 as an aid in your writing.

When confronted with this problem in supervision, Allan embarked on a journey that caused him to reflect on his underlying assumptions. He approached the problem with double-loop learning in mind and recognised how he had brought conflicting values into the room (see Figure 8.3). He had, for instance, nourished an omnipotent fantasy of being expected – and able – to 'save' all marriages that came his way. His own personal experiences were brought into the room in addition to his moral and cultural values that suggest that divorce ought to be avoided at all cost.

ACTIVITY 8.1

- Identify a problem that you feel prevents your practice from moving forward.
- Consider it from both a single-loop and a double-loop learning perspective. What may have influenced your failed strategy?
- Try to identify some key differences between your espoused theory – what you set out to do – and your theory-in-use – what actually happened. Use your underlying personal, socio-cultural and theoretical thoughts and actions to describe what influences this outcome.

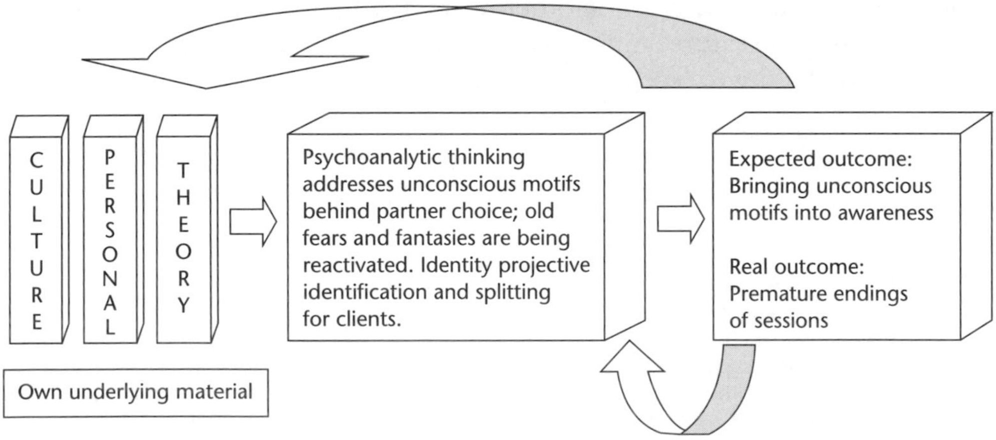

Figure 8.3: Outcomes: double-loop learning

ACT SMART

This section focuses on the actual outcomes of reflective learning. Reflective learning involves moving from noticing a problem to transforming it into something of practical use. Reflective practice is ultimately about 'harnessing' this process, by moving it from tacit, implicit knowledge to an explicit level where both you and others can evaluate your strategies.

REFLECTION POINT

As is the case with all qualitative research and inquiry, if reflective learning cannot be documented and evaluated by others, it fails to keep its status as a reliable and informative inquiry. A need to redefine objectivity should not be confused with a disregard for systematic inquiry.

To say that 'objectivity is constructed' (Parker, 2004) does not mean that its objectivity is unimportant or that 'anything goes'. The claim rests on the belief that it *is* important to recognise and share *how* understandings and meaning making processes are constructed.

- Think about Parker's criteria for 'good' research as grounded, coherent and accessible.

To help you with your reflective practice, an understanding of the model referred to as ACT SMART is important.

The ACT model comprises five outcomes and levels of reflective learning:

- acknowledging/noticing;
- considering/making sense;
- connecting/making meaning;
- transforming into theory/working with meaning;
- transforming into practice.

Each level builds on the knowledge and insight required in the preceding level.

The SMART model is borrowed from Roffey-Barentsen and Malthouse (2009) and refers to an action plan that can assist you in setting 'measurable' goals and to make your inquiry coherent and accessible. SMART stands for:

- Specific;
- Measurable;

- Achievable;
- Relevant;
- Time-bound.

IDENTIFY YOUR NEEDS

The point of your own reflective practice manifesto is to support you in making an assessment of your own needs, with subsequent actions in mind. You are encouraged to engage with your supervisor in the first instance, but also to consider other options in terms of personal therapy, peer groups and further reading and/or training. It is also a requirement for accreditation and registration as a practitioner. The BACP and the UKCP require 'evidence' of reflective practice, and the ACT SMART model can help you to 'know and utilise' your problem situations.

The boundaries between personal, cultural and theoretical underlying assumptions are often fleeting. In the case study about Allan, for instance, the theory-in-use that triggers a 'saviour' stance towards all his clients could be related to personal, educational *and* ethical issues. It is nevertheless important to pinpoint separate themes. These are, in turn, helpful when considering a 'measurable' action plan that can be evaluated by yourself and others:

- your *personal* needs such as personal therapy and peer groups;
- your *educational* needs in terms of further reading, workshops, training and general CPD (continuing professional development);
- the implications of *ethical and professional* requirements, which will prompt you to reconsider boundaries, such as those relating to confidentiality, on an ongoing basis – what do you need to do to meet these requirements?

Below is an explanation of the ACT SMART models with reference to Allan, from the case study about couple counselling. Consider your own problem while reading. You may wish to scribble or underline as you read, before you begin to fill in the form at the end of the text.

ACT SMART

Step 1: Acknowledging/noticing

Something is wrong but you do not know exactly what. Roffey-Barentsen (2009: 17) compares it to the breakdown of a car. At this stage, the level of understanding can be compared with 'knowing the names of some parts of a car'.

Example

Allan notices that something is 'wrong' when confronted by his supervisor about the recurring patterns of prematurely discontinued sessions. Not surprisingly, he feels insulted, misunderstood and deskilled. His intention to 'help' couples by saving marriages was maybe never really at the forefront of his mind, but he recognises now in supervision how strong his need to save marriages has actually been. On his way home he experiences a great sense of resentment towards his supervisor whom he feels is cold and uncaring; does she not realise what pain divorce can cause to families, children, single dads? His own experience of divorce surfaces again. The pain of divorce is accompanied by a sense of failure at work.

Step 2: Considering/making sense

This is a stage when tentative connections are made and tried out. Roffey-Barentsen and Malthouse (2009) continue:

> *[some] pieces of knowledge are identified but these are tenuous and lack comprehension or awareness. Now it is realised that the steering wheel controls the wheels in some way.*

Example

As a therapist, Allan explores the 'problem' on several levels. He recalls what he learnt in personal therapy about identifying strong reactions; he identifies that the overwhelming sense of failure is a familiar one, something that he has explored many times before. For a single child with a mother suffering regular bouts of depression, powerlessness is a familiar feeling. No matter what he did his mother would occasionally sink into deep pockets of depression. This used to leave him both alone, useless and unloved. Just like now. Allan is surprised at his own reaction; he thought he 'had dealt with all this'. He begins to consider the option of contacting the therapist again but is at this stage primarily relieved over the connection he has made between his strong feelings with reference to actual events. He is beginning to recognise a discrepancy between his psychodynamic framework and the need to save marriages. The supervisor had a point. The whole thing feels less personal now. Allan begins to consider reading up some more about the therapeutic relationship in couple counselling. He can see the role that his underlying personal involvement has played in the problem and he also recognises that he is newly qualified. He feels keen to gain more knowledge.

Action plan, level 1

A tentative action plan takes shape as his desire to learn more about the problems increases. He is not ready to make specific plans. His own personal therapy and further training are tentative options.

Step 3: Connecting/making meaning

Further connections are being made 'but not enough to make claim to full comprehension', as Roffey-Barentsen and Malthouse (2009) put it. They write:

> *The relationship between the steering wheel, steering column, axle and wheels has been identified; however, there is no knowledge of differential or the rack and pinion. If this person were given the parts of a car to put together it is unlikely that anything other than modern art would be produced.*

Example

Allan reads whatever he can as he is uncertain about where to start in order to understand more about the role of couple counsellor. His previous training seems to have prepared him for textbook cases. In reality all cases are different. He feels confused and the sessions feel more like riding bareback on a wild horse; he notices things in the room in a new way and it feels very busy, often out of control. He starts to make notes in a new way; he needs to separate the voices and the unspoken messages in the room. He makes mind maps and is beginning to find a way of writing about the sessions afterwards, which helps him to reflect. He has got two piles of books that he dips into: one pile is about countertransference and the therapist's own reaction and the other pile is about counselling in general. Perhaps the psychodynamic model wasn't for him? He wants to learn more about different options.

Action plan, level 2

This stage of Allan's action plan involves brainstorming, skimming through as much material as possible and recognising themes and areas of particular relevance to his problem. He is considering whether or not to return to the same therapist as before or to contact a new therapist. He consults different directories, which help him to specify to himself what he wants to work with at this stage of his life. What has he learnt? What areas would he benefit from exploring further? He underlines, scribbles and is beginning to make entries in a separate new notebook. He is beginning to feel a sense of pride in his profession return. Allan recognises that part of his action plan revolves at this stage around managing change.

Managing change

Managing change usually involves confronting a loss of self, or at least the loss of elements that made up parts of what we used to be in terms of attitudes, habits and/or deep-seated values about ourselves or others.

As suggested earlier, to question one's own stance is inevitably a part of the process involved in trying on new perspectives. In the case of Allan, his role as a 'saviour' stems from a stage in life when 'saving' developed as a protection against losing his mother through bouts of depression. Supporting and 'saving' made him feel cared for; it brought more time with his mother. His own subsequent failed marriage feeds easily into Allan's sense of loss with regard to relationships. As Allan explores his own underlying agenda for 'saving' couples he recognises that the underpinning aim has been to 'save' himself, i.e. to maintain a sense of identity and direction.

Tschudi's ABC model is inspired by George Kelly (1955), one of the earliest constructivists within psychology. Kelly suggested that often, without really thinking about it, we base our understanding of 'reality' on prior personal experiences. Banister et al. (1994: 85) describe the rationale behind the model as follows:

> *Often we fail again and again to achieve the personal claim to want to make. The ABC model devised by Tschudi is particularly useful for revealing possible underlying tensions (core constructs) that prevent us from making the change . . . revealing personal implications in this way can highlight why a person is 'stuck' and offer new understanding of the dilemma which enables them to begin to make changes, to reconstruct, if that is what they choose to do.*

Rather than actually assessing the present, Kelly suggested that we obscured our view with anticipatory constructs based on experience from before. In Table 8.1, Allan gets the opportunity to 'unpick' and gain a deeper understanding into what 'saving' versus 'flexibility' actually means to him. Once he recognises the negative experiences he is transferring from the past, he is able to reconsider the situation and reconstruct the meaning that saving and being flexible may be given.

Step 4: Transforming into theory/abstracting, working with meaning

The parts are beginning to fit in with the whole. Roffey-Barentsen and Malthouse (2009) write:

> *The person has a clear idea of the name and function of each component part of the car and can identify the existing relationships between each part and the car.*

A1 Present position	A2 Preferred position
• Allan is confronted in supervision for being rigid (always using the same homework on clients) and approaching clients with his own agenda (saving all marriages)	• Allan and his supervisor agree that Allan could be more flexible with less need to 'save'
B1 Disadvantages of present position	**B2 Advantages of preferred position**
• Clients are discontinuing sessions prematurely • Allan feels frustrated with all clients • Allan often despairs about work • Feeling totally responsible for others is stressful, exhausting	• Not 'saving' could pave way for a more equal relationship with clients • Not carrying all responsibility would be a relief • Not 'saving' would move Allan's role into a more professional place • Being more flexible and open to others' agendas could improve work; clients may stay longer and actually get 'stuck into' work
C1 Advantages of present position	**C2 Disadvantages of preferred position**
• Saving feels like a 'safe', known place. It is what you do to be appreciated • Saving gives Allan a sense of identity and direction • Saving others puts Allan in control (it is their loss if they leave)	• Not saving can be dangerous. God knows what can happen if Allan doesn't keep others on track (they might get depressed, like mother) • Not saving requires a whole not set of skills – a new approach to life, even. Can he muster the challenge?

Table 8.1: The ABC model reveals underlying tensions between core constructs

Example

Allan's separate new notebook consists now of a comprehensive list of his own special interests and needs. Specific books are referenced and listed, interesting workshops have been planned or booked, and arrangements with a personal therapist have been made, for a time-limited period initially. His interest in the therapeutic relationship in couple counselling feels justified, partly given his newly qualified status. He has also Googled the subject area enough to realise that some themes are under-represented in the literature he has found. He discusses the issue with his supervisor who agrees, and she invites him to instigate a peer group around the topic within the agency.

Action plan, level 3

Allan's problem-solving plan is now put into action. It is up and running. His action plan can be referred to as SMART in the sense that Roffey-Barentsen and Malthouse use the term. It is an action plan that is:

- *Specific* – Allan wants to learn more about the therapeutic relationship in couple counselling, with a initial specific focus on countertransference.
- *Measurable* – a schedule is set for personal therapy, workshop attendance and further training; Allan has received interest in his peer group, which can start within a couple of weeks; and he senses a direction with regard to the reading he aims to undertake over the next year.
- *Achievable* – Allan's commitments feel carefully considered and are planned to fit into his other obligations such as his children, who stay with him every second week.
- *Time-bound* – the workshops and personal therapy are something that Allan approaches with a time limit in mind; he wants to apply for a year-long course and has got his supervisor's support to make the application.

Step 5: Transforming into practice

This is the stage of learning where the initial problem has become an asset, something to be incorporated as a valuable experience, almost like 'recycling' something that was previously useless. It can be compared with wisdom and deep insight, where the learner 'is able to make connections with the specific subject matter and has the ability to go beyond it' (Roffey-Barentsen and Malthouse, 2009: 17). They continue:

> *[The learner] can take a broad view and transfer principles and ideas to other subject knowledge areas. The person can relate their knowledge of a specific car to that of other cars, mini buses, vans etc.*

Example

Thanks to his experiences in supervision when confronted with the problem of discontinued sessions and when recognising an underlying attempt to 'save' all the marriages that came in his way, Allan is able to admit to and recognise blind spots. The fact that he thought he did one thing but seems to do another overwhelmed him at first. Now, it seems human. He has read up enough on the subject to realise just how complex sessions can be when three people meet at a crossroads, as in the case of a pending divorce. All sorts of things will surface. The therapist's own reactions are essential to consider, but something that Allan has accepted that some agencies and training programmes expect the therapist to take on themselves to pursue insights into. The lesson that Allan sees as most valuable to have learnt through his own raw experiences accompanied by his subsequent systematic 're-search' into the problem is that 'not knowing' may be one of the most valuable contributions a therapist can offer. Rather than pressing homework and solutions on to the clients, as before, Allan is comfortable with ambivalence – his own and the clients'. He regards it as his job to offer his clients the space to explore and find their own meaning to relationships, marriage and divorce. Coming to terms with ambivalence has helped Allan to adopt a much more flexible and open stance during the sessions. He makes a point of picking up signals from the clients if and when he instigates his own interventions; what may work with one couple may be inappropriate or irrelevant for others. Reflection-in-practice becomes in this sense an important part of Allan's work; he is more ready to stop in his tracks and change tack, in response to the interaction in the room. He feels that the problem addressed in supervision has helped him to become a better listener.

ACTIVITY 8.2

Return to your initial 'tentative checklist' from Chapter 1.

Reconsider the questions below and your own earlier replies. Make a new list of at least five examples for each theme.

- Your *normative* needs. In what ways can you assess and consider your practice with regard to professional and ethical guidelines, norms and laws?
- Your *formative* needs. In what ways can you receive feedback or direction in order to develop skills, theoretical knowledge and personal attributes as a practitioner?
- Your *restorative* needs. How are you listened to, supported, confronted and challenged with regard to your personal issues, doubts and insecurities?

What stands out to you about yourself and your needs? If you have identified an 'area for change' but feel uncertain about how to narrow down the dilemma or 'problem', you are advised to explore the issue in the context of the ABC model. Once you feel that you have narrowed down the 'problem', go on to the next activity, with your ACT SMART plan.

ACTIVITY 8.3

- Use this activity as a kind of self-assessment, to narrow down and identify your needs relating to, for instance, CPD (continuous professional development), supervision, personal therapy and peer support. This stage represents the final level of your writing – the stage that Smith (1985: 127) calls 're-writing'.
- Explore a recurring issue of your own, following the ACT SMART steps used in the example with Allan. In summary, these are:

Step 1 Acknowledging/noticing: something is wrong – describe what it looks like, feels like and where it takes place.

Step 2 Considering/making sense: make and try out tentative connections.

Action plan, level 1: make a tentative action plan.

Step 3: Connecting/making meaning: describe the tentative connections you are making.

Action plan, level 2: brainstorm ideas, do research on areas of relevance to your problem.

Managing change: discuss how to manage change with your supervisor and your peers, and maybe use the ABC model in your thinking.

Step 4: Transforming into theory: begin to fit the parts into the whole.

Action plan, level 3: finalise your plan so that it is ready to be put into action – prepare to discuss your steps with reference to the SMART stages.

Step 5: Transforming into practice: describe how your problem will be transformed, 'recycled' into something useful and valuable for your practice. What have you learnt? How will this be used? How does your recycled knowledge benefit your client and thereby yourself as a good enough practitioner?

CHAPTER SUMMARY

- This chapter has been about you and your own reflective manifesto. There are no obvious rights or wrongs in reflective practice – rather, a considerable number of guidelines. This chapter pursues the thinking about systematic inquiry with reference to different models and learning cycles.
- You have been encouraged to complete your own reflective practice manifesto. This involves distinguishing a part in your notebook for 'rewriting', i.e. revisiting your own writing and responding to it as if written by someone else.

- The first step is to 'rewrite' about yourself, with your own personal, socio-cultural and theoretical values, beliefs and assumptions in mind. As a reminder, return to 'Sofie's story' in the Preface.
- Next, you are encouraged to identify a 'problem' that affects your practice. The ABC model might help you to structure your thoughts.
- You have been able to follow Allan through his ACT SMART process and are expected to write your own ACT SMART inquiry.
- Your ACT SMART inquiry will be subject to input, feedback and different forms of support. You are expected to discuss your identified needs and action plan with your supervisor in the first place.
- Professionals within the 'helping professions' rely on each other to evidence good practice. People put a great trust in our services. It is usually with pride and shared joy that we feel that clients were right in trusting us. To support others, we need help and support ourselves. This book encourages you to take your needs seriously and to ACT SMART with them. Good luck!

SUGGESTED FURTHER READING

Barber, P (2006) *Becoming a practitioner researcher: a gestalt approach to holistic inquiry*. London: Middlesex University Press.

This is a good introduction for those with an interest in work-based learning. Barber approaches research in a similar way to Simon's, with a demystifying approach where the complexity of human beings and life is taken into account.

Moon, J (2004) *A handbook of reflective and experiential learning: theory and practice*. London: Routledge.

Jennifer Moon adopts a methodical, integrated approach to reflective and experiential learning. The book is aimed at teachers in particular, but is useful for anyone who wants to develop and use reflective and experiential learning . The book includes useful models and provides practical advice, tools, activities and photocopiable resources that can be incorporated into your practice.

Roffey-Barentsen, J and Malthouse, R (2009) *Reflective practice in the lifelong learning sector*. Exeter: Learning Matters.

This book is filled with practical and accessible guidance to the reflective learning process and recommended to those seeking a hands-on approach to the topic.

Appendix

Clinical Outcomes in Routine Evaluation (CORE)

For more information on CORE Information Management Systems go to **www.coreims.co.uk.**

CLINICAL
OUTCOMES in
ROUTINE
EVALUATION

OUTCOME MEASURE

Site ID

letters only numbers only

Client ID

Therapist ID numbers only (1) numbers only (2)

Sub codes

D D / M M / Y Y Y Y

Date form given

Age

Male

Female

Stage Completed

S Screening
R Referral
A Assessment
F First Therapy Session
P Pre-therapy (unspecified)
D During Therapy
L Last therapy session
X Follow up 1
Y Follow up 2

Stage

Episode

IMPORTANT - PLEASE READ THIS FIRST

This form has 34 statements about how you have been OVER THE LAST WEEK.
Please read each statement and think how often you felt that way last week.
Then tick the box which is closest to this.
Please use a dark pen (not pencil) and tick clearly within the boxes.

	Over the last week	Not at all	Only Occasionally	Sometimes	Often	Most or all the time	OFFICE USE ONLY
1	I have felt terribly alone and isolated	0	1	2	3	4	F
2	I have felt tense, anxious or nervous	0	1	2	3	4	P
3	I have felt I have someone to turn to for support when needed	4	3	2	1	0	F
4	I have felt O.K. about myself	4	3	2	1	0	W
5	I have felt totally lacking in energy and enthusiasm	0	1	2	3	4	P
6	I have been physically violent to others	0	1	2	3	4	R
7	I have felt able to cope when things go wrong	4	3	2	1	0	F
8	I have been troubled by aches, pains or other physical problems	0	1	2	3	4	P
9	I have thought of hurting myself	0	1	2	3	4	R
10	Talking to people has felt too much for me	0	1	2	3	4	F
11	Tension and anxiety have prevented me doing important things	0	1	2	3	4	P
12	I have been happy with the things I have done.	4	3	2	1	0	F
13	I have been disturbed by unwanted thoughts and feelings	0	1	2	3	4	P
14	I have felt like crying	0	1	2	3	4	W

Please turn over

Survey : 151 Page : 1

Over the last week

		Not at all	Only Occasionally	Sometimes	Often	Most or all the time	OFFICE USE ONLY
15	I have felt panic or terror	0	1	2	3	4	P
16	I made plans to end my life	0	1	2	3	4	R
17	I have felt overwhelmed by my problems	0	1	2	3	4	W
18	I have had difficulty getting to sleep or staying asleep	0	1	2	3	4	P
19	I have felt warmth or affection for someone	4	3	2	1	0	F
20	My problems have been impossible to put to one side	0	1	2	3	4	P
21	I have been able to do most things I needed to	4	3	2	1	0	F
22	I have threatened or intimidated another person	0	1	2	3	4	R
23	I have felt despairing or hopeless	0	1	2	3	4	P
24	I have thought it would be better if I were dead	0	1	2	3	4	R
25	I have felt criticised by other people	0	1	2	3	4	F
26	I have thought I have no friends	0	1	2	3	4	F
27	I have felt unhappy	0	1	2	3	4	P
28	Unwanted images or memories have been distressing me	0	1	2	3	4	P
29	I have been irritable when with other people	0	1	2	3	4	F
30	I have thought I am to blame for my problems and difficulties	0	1	2	3	4	P
31	I have felt optimistic about my future	4	3	2	1	0	W
32	I have achieved the things I wanted to	4	3	2	1	0	F
33	I have felt humiliated or shamed by other people	0	1	2	3	4	F
34	I have hurt myself physically or taken dangerous risks with my health	0	1	2	3	4	R

THANK YOU FOR YOUR TIME IN COMPLETING THIS QUESTIONNAIRE

	(W)	(P)	(F)	(R)	All items	All minus R
Total Scores						
Mean Scores (Total score for each dimension divided by number of items completed in that dimension)						

Survey : 151 Page : 2

References

Adorno, TW, Frenkel-Brunswik, E, Levinson, DJ and Sanford, RN (1989) The authoritarian personality, in Bronner, S and Kellner, D. (eds) *Critical theory and society – a reader*. London: Routledge.

Alvesson, M and Skoldeberg, K (2000) *Reflexive methodology*. London: Sage.

Argyris, M and Schön, D (1974) *Theory in practice: increasing professional effectiveness*. San Francisco CA: Jossey-Bass.

Argyris, C and Schön, D (1978) *Organizational learning: a theory of action perspective*. Reading MA: Addison Wesley.

Argyris, C, Putnam, R and Smith, D (1985) *Action science: concepts, methods and skills for research intervention*. San Francisco CA: Jossey-Bass.

Atherton, JS (2009) *Learning and teaching: SOLO taxonomy*. Online. Available at www.learningandteaching.info/learning/solo.htm.

Aujoulat, I, Luminet, O and Deccache, A (2007) The perspective of patients on their experience of powerlessness. *Qualitative Health Research*, 17 (6): 772–85.

Bager-Charleson, S (2003) *The parent's school? Narrative research about parental involvement in school*. Lund: University of Lund.

Bager-Charleson, S (2010) *Why do therapists choose to be therapists*? London: Karnac Books.

Bain, R (1997). Survival, in Horton, I and Varma, V (eds), *The needs of counsellors and psychotherapists*. London: Sage.

Bannister, P, Burman, E, Parker, I, Taylor, M and Tindall, C (1994) *Qualitative methods in psychology: a research guide*. Buckingham: Open University Press.

Bannister, B and Fransella, F (1986) *Inquiring man: the psychology of personal constructs*, 3rd ed. London: Croom Helm.

Barber, P (2006) *Becoming a practitioner researcher: a gestalt approach to holistic inquiry*. London: Middlesex University Press.

Barkham, M and Hardy, GE (2001) Counselling and interpersonal therapies for depression: towards securing an evidence-base. *British Medical Bulletin*, 57: 115–32.

Bärmark, J and Nilsson, I (1983) *Poul Bjerre-Människonen*. Borås: Natur och Kultur.

Bateman, A and Holmes, J (1999) *Introduction to psychoanalysis: contemporary theory and practice*. London: Brunner Routledge.

Behar, R (1996) *The vulnerable observer: anthropology that breaks your heart*. Boston MA: Beacon Press.

Berne, E (1964) *Games people play*. New York: Grove Press.

Bernstein, R (ed) (1988) *Habermas and modernity*. Oxford: Polity Press.

Biggs, J and Collis, K (1982) *Evaluating the quality of learning: the SOLO taxonomy*. New York: Academic Press.

Billig, M (1997) Freud and Dora: repressing an oppressed identity. *Theory, Culture and Society*, 14: 29–55.

Bion, W (1962) *Learning from experience*. London: Karnak.

Bollas, C (1987) *The shadow of the object: psychoanalysis of the unthought known*. London: Free Association Books.

Bolton, G (2005) *Reflective practice – writing and professional development*. London: Sage.

Bond, T (2000) *Standards and ethics for counselling in action*. London: Sage.

Bond, T (2004) *Ethical guidelines for researching counselling and psychotherapy*. Rugby: BACP.

Borgatti, SP (1996) *Bureaucracy: introduction to organizational behaviour 2001*. Boston MA: Boston College.

Boud, D and Solomon, N (2003) *Work-based learning: a new higher education?* Buckingham: Open University Press.

Bowlby, J (1969) *Attachment*. London: Pelican.

Broden, M (2005) Developmental theories in the process of change, in Safvestad Nolan, I and Nolan, P (eds) *Object relations and integrative psychotherapy: tradition and innovation in theory and practice*. London: Whurr Publishers.

Bronner, S and Kellner, D (1989) *Critical theory and society: a reader*. London: Routledge.

Brown, K and Butter, L (2008) *Critical thinking for social work*. Hove: Learning Matters.

Brown, RA and Levinsohn, PM (1984) A psychoeducational approach to the treatment of depression: comparison of the group, individual and minimal contact procedures. *Journal of Consulting and Clinical Psychology*, 52 (5): 774–83.

Bruner, J (1990) *Acts of meaning*. Cambridge MA: Harvard University Press.

Buber, M (1947/1971) *Between man & man*. Glasgow: Fontana Library.

Bury, M (1991) The sociology of chronic illness: a review of research and prospects. *Sociology of Health and Illness*, 13 (4): 451–68.

Cardinal, D, Hayward, J and Jones, G (2005) *Epistemology: the theory of knowledge*. London: Hodder Murray.

Carter, D and Gradin, S (2001) *Writing as reflective action: a reader*. New York: LongmanPearson.

Casement, P (2008a) *Learning from life: becoming a psychoanalyst*. London: Routledge.

Casement, P (2008b) *Learning from our mistakes: beyond dogma in psychoanalysis and psychotherapy*. New York: Psychology Press.

Cashdan, S (1988) *Object relation therapy: using the relationship*. Ontario: Penguin Books.

Chang, LC, Li, IC and Liu, CH (2004) A study of the empowerment process for cancer patients using Freire's dialogical interviewing. *Journal of Nursing Research*, 12 (1), 41–49.

Charmaz, K (1983) Loss of self: a fundamental form of suffering in the chronically ill. *Sociology of Health and Illness*, 5 (2), 168–95.

Charon, R (2006). *Narrative medicine: honouring the stories of illness*. New York: Oxford University Press.

Chenail, RJ (1994) Qualitative research and clinical work: 'private-ization' and 'public-ation' [39 paragraphs]. *The Qualitative Report*. Online serial, 2 (1). Available at http://www.nova.edu/ssss/QR/BackIssues/QR2–1/private.html.

Chenail, RJ and Maione, P (1997). Sensemaking in clinical qualitative research [28 paragraphs]. *The Qualitative Report*. On-line serial, 3 (1). Available at http:// www.nova.edu/ssss/QR/QR3–1/sense.html.

Chernin, K (1994) *The hungry self: women, eating, and identity*. New York: HarperPerennial.

Clark, JN and James, S (2003) The radicalized self: the impact on the self of the contested nature of the diagnosis of chronic fatigue syndrome. *Social Science and Medicine*, 57 (8): 1387–95.

Clarkson, P (2002) *The therapeutic relationship*. London: Whurr.

Cooper, M (2008) *Essential research findings in counselling and psychotherapy: the facts are friendly*. Glasgow: Sage Publications.

Corbin, J and Strauss, A (1987) Accompaniments of chronic illness: changes in body, self, biography, and biological time. *Research in the Sociology of Health Care*, 6: 249–81.

Cozolino, L (2002) *The neuroscience of psychotherapy building and rebuilding the human brain*. London: Norton.

Crossley, M (2000) *Introducing narrative psychology: self, trauma and the construction of meaning*. Buckingham: Open University Press.

Crossley, N (2000) *Reflexive embodiment in contemporary society*. Maidenhead: Open University Press.

Dallos, R and Miell, D (1996) *Social interaction and personal relationships*. London: Sage.

Davies, HTO (2004) *What works? Evidence-based policy and practice in public service*. Bristol: Policy Press.

Davies, M (2007) *Boundaries in counselling and psychotherapy*. Twickenham: Athena Press.

Despenser, S (2007) Risk assessment: the personal safety of the counselor. *Therapy Today*, March: 12–13.

Drozd, JF and Goldfried, MR (1996). A critical evaluation of the state-of-the-art in Psychotherapy Outcome Research. *Psychotherapy: Theory, Research, Practice, Training*. Summer, 33 (2): 171–80.

du Plock, S (2004) What do we mean when we use the word 'research'? *Existential Analysis*, 15 (1): 29–37.

Ellis, JHM and Kiely, JA (2000) Action inquiry strategies: taking stock and moving forward. *Journal of Applied Management Studies*, 9 (1): 83–94.

Etherington, K (1995) *Adult male survivors of childhood abuse*. Brighton: Pavilion Publishing.

Etherington, K (2004) *Becoming a reflexive researcher: using our selves in research*. London: Jessica Kingsley.

Fairbairn, WRD (1952) *Psychoanalytic study of the personality*. New York: Taylor & Francis.

Finlay, L and Gough, B (2003) *Reflexivity: a practical guide for researchers in health and social science*. London: Blackwell.

Fonagy, P, Gergeley, G, Jurist, EJ and Target, MI (2002) *Affect regulation, mentalization, and the development of the self*. New York: Other Press.

Fook, J (2002) *Social work: critical theory and practice*. London: Sage.

Fook, J and Pease, B (1999) *Transforming social work practice: postmodern critical perspectives*. London: Routledge.

Foucault, M (1984) The Birth of the Asylum in Madness and Civilisation 1961, in Rabinow, P (ed) *The Foucault reader: the introduction to Foucault's thoughts*. London: Penguin Books.

Freud, S (1938/1959) *An outline of psycho-analysis*, London: The Hogarth Press.

Freud, S (1961) New introductory lectures on psychoanalysis, vol 2, Strachey, J (ed). Middlesex: Penguin Books.

Freud, S (1963) *Dora: an analysis of a case of hysteria*, Rieff, P (ed). New York: Collier.

Freud, S (1991), Introductory lectures on psychoanalysis, vol 1, Strachey, J (ed). Middlesex: Penguin Books.

Friedman, VJ (2001). Action science: creating communities of inquiry in communities of practice, in Reason, P and Bradbury, H (eds) *Handbook of action research: participative inquiry and practice*. London: Sage Publications, pp 150–70.

Frommer, J and Langenbach, M (2001) The psychoanalytic case study as a source of epistemic knowledge, in Frommer, J and Rennie, D (eds) *Qualitative psychotherapy research methods and methodology*. Lengerich: Pabst Science Publishers.

Frommer, J and Rennie, D (eds) (2001) *Qualitative psychotherapy research methods and methodology*. Lengerich: Pabst Science Publishers.

Gadamer, HG (1989) *Truth and method*. New York: Crossroad.

Gardner, F (2008) Using critical reflection in research and evaluation, in White, S, Fook, J and Gardner, F (eds) *Critical reflection in health and social care*. Maidenhead: Open University Press, pp 156–72.

Gay, P (ed) (1989) *Sigmund Freud: civilization and its discontents*. London: Norton & Company.

Gay, P (ed) (1995) *The Freud reader*. London: Vintage.

Gergen, K (1989) The possibility of psychological knowledge: a hermeneutic inquiry, in Packer, MJ, Addison, RB (eds) *Entering the circle: hermeneutic investigation in psychology*. New York: State University of New York.

Gergen, K (1998) Narrative, moral identity and historical consciousness: a social constructionist account, Straub, J (ed). Suhrkamp, Frankfurt, read as draft for volume on narrative for University of Bielefeld.

Gergen, K (2009) *An invitation to social constructionism* (2nd ed). New York: Sage.

Gergen, K and Gergen, M (1986) Narrative form and the construction of Psychological Science, in Polkinghorne, D (1988) *Narrative knowing and the human sciences*. New York: Suny.

Gergen, K and Graumann, C (2006) *Historical dimensions of psychological discourses*. Cambridge: Cambridge University Press.

Gergen, M (1997) *Towards a new psychology of gender*. New York: Routledge.

Ghaemi, SN (2007) *The concepts of psychiatry; a pluralistic approach to the mind and mental illness*. Baltimore MD: Johns Hopkins University Press.

Gibbs, G (1988) *Learning by doing: a guide to teaching and learning methods*. Oxford: Oxford Brookes University Further Education Unit.

Giddens, A (1988) Reason without revolution? in Bernstein, R (ed) *Habermas and modernity*. Oxford: Polity Press.

Grassie, W (1994) Reinventing nature: science narratives as myths for an endangered planet. Dissertation. Philadelphia PA: Temple University.

Greco-Brooks, DM (2003) Feeding identity: The critical hermeneutics of contemporary Kleinian psychoanalytically orientated psychotherapy from the perspective of a novice. PhD Dissertation, Faculty of Psychology, Dallas TX: University Duquesne.

Green, V (ed) (2008) *Emotional development in psychoanalysis, attachment theory and neuroscience*. London and New York: Routledge.

Greenberg, M, Shergill, SS, Szmukler, G and Tantam, D (2003) *Narratives in psychiatry*. London: Jessica Kingsley.

Greenwood, D and Loewenthal, D (2005) The use of 'case-study' in psychotherapeutic research and education. *Psychoanalytic Psychotherapy Journal*, 19:1–13.

Guggenbuhl-Craig, A (1991) Quacks, charlatans and false prophets, in Sweig, C and Abrams, J (eds) *Meeting the shadow*. New York: Penguin group.

Guggenbuhl-Craig, A (2009) *Power in the helping professions*. Putnam CT: Spring Publications.

Habermas, J (1973) *Theory and practice*. Cambridge: Polity Press.

Habermas, J (1987) *The theory of communicative action*, vol 2. Boston MA: Beacon Press.

Hall, S (1996) Reflexivity in emancipatory action research: illustrating the researcher's constitutiveness, in Zuber-Skerritt, O (ed) *New directions in action research*. London: Falmer Press.

Hargaden, H and Sills, C (2002) *Transactional analysis: a relational perspective*. New York: Brunner-Routledge.

Hawkins, P and Shohet, R (2008) *Supervision in the helping professions*. Maidenhead: Open University Press.

Healey, K. (2005) *Social work theories in context: creating frameworks for practice*. New York: Palgrave Macmillan.

Heron, J and Reason, P (2001) The practice of co-operative inquiry, in Reason, P and Bradbury, H (eds) *Handbook of action research: participative inquiry and practice*. London: Sage Publications, pp 179–88.

Holloway, W and Featherstone, B (eds) (1997) *Mothering and ambivalence*. London and New York: Routledge.

Holloway, W and Jefferson, T (2002) *Doing qualitative research differently: free association, narrative and the interview method*. London and New Delhi: Sage.

Holmes, J and Bateman, A (2002) *Integration in psychotherapy models and methods*. Oxford: Oxford University Press.

Holmes, J and Lindley, R (1998) *The values of psychotherapy*. London: Karnac Books.

Hoshmand, LT and Polkinghorne, DE (1992) Redefining the science–practice relationship and professional training, education and training. *Psychology*, 47 (1): 55–66.

Hunt, C (2000) *Therapeutic dimensions of autobiography in creative writing*. London: Jessica Kingsley.

Hunt, C and Sampson, F (eds) (2002) *The self on the page: theory and practice of creative writing in personal development*. London: Jessica Kingsley.

Ingram, D (1997) The narrative perspective in dynamic psychiatry. Presentation to the Society of Medical Psychoanalysts.

Jenkins, P (2007) *Counselling, psychotherapy and the law*, (2nd ed). London: Sage.

Jones-Devitt, S and Smith, L (2007) *Critical thinking in health and social care*. London: Sage.

Josselson, R (ed) (1996) *Ethics and process in the narrative study of lives*. London: Sage.

Kagan, N (1967). Studies in human interaction: interpersonal process recall stimulated by videotape. East Lansing MI: Michigan State University, East Lansing College of Education.

Kalsched, D (1996) *The inner world of trauma: archetypal defenses of the personal spirit*. Hove and New York: Brunner-Routledge.

Kant, I (1781/2007) *Critique of pure reason*, revised ed. London: Penguin Books Classics.

Kelly, GA (1955) *The psychology of personal constructs*. New York: Norton

King's College Chronic Fatigue (CFS) Research and Treatment Unit (2007). Website available at www.kcl.ac.uk/projects/cfs/referrals.html.

Klein, M (1988) *Love, guilt and reparation: and other works 1921–1947*. London: Virago Press.

Knott, C and Scragg, T (2008) *Reflective practice in social work*. Exeter: Learning Matters.

Kristeva, J (1989) *Tales of love*, Roudiez, L (trans). London: Free Association Books.

Kvale, S (ed) (1999) *Psychology and postmodernism*. London: Sage.

Kvale, S (2001) The psychoanalytic interview as qualitative research, in Frommer, J and Rennie, D (eds) *Qualitative psychotherapy research methods and methodology*. Lengerich: Pabst Science Publishers.

Lacan, J (1977) *Ecrits: a selection*, Sheridan, Alain (trans). London: Tavistock Publications.

Lebow, J (2007) *Research for the psychotherapist: from science to practice*. Abingdon: Routledge.

Lieblich, A, Tuval-Mashiach, R and Zilber, T (1998) *Narrative research: reading, analysis and interpretations*. London: Sage.

Lieblich, A, Josselson, R and McAdams, DP (2001) *Turns in the road: narrative studies of lives in transition*. American Psychological Association.

Loewenthal, D and Snell, R (2003) *Post-modernism for psychotherapists*. Hove: Brunner & Routledge.

Loewenthal, D and Winter, D (2006) *What is Therapeutic Research?* London: Karnac.

Luborsky, L, Crits-Christophy, P, Mintz, J and Aurbach, A (1988) *Who will benefit from psychotherapy? Predicting therapeutic outcomes*. New York: Basic Books.

Lyotard, J (1986) *The postmodern condition: a report on knowledge*, Bennington, G (trans). Manchester: Manchester University Press.

Malcolm, J (1081) *Psychoanalysis: the impossible profession*. New York: First Vintage Books.

Margison, FR, Barkham, M, Evans, C, McGrath, G, Mellor-Clark, J, Audin, K and Connell, J (2000). Measurement and psychotherapy evidence-based practice and practice based evidence. *British Journal of Psychiatry*, 177: 123–30.

May, R, Angel, E and Ellenberger, HF (eds) (1979) *Existence: a new dimension in psychiatry and psychology*. New York: Basic Books.

McAdams, D (1993) *The stories we live by: personal myths and the making of the self*. New York: The Guilford Press.

McLeod, J (1994) *Doing counselling research*. London: Sage.

McLeod, J (1997) Research and evaluation in counselling, in Palmer, S (ed) *1997 handbook of counselling*, 2nd ed, London: Routledge.

McLeod, J (1999) *Practitioner research in counselling*. London: Sage

McLeod, J (2001) *Qualitative research in counselling and psychotherapy*. London and New Delhi: Sage.

McLeod, J and Balamoutsou, S (2001) A method for qualitative narrative analysis of psychotherapy transcripts, in Mearns, D and Thorne, B *Person-centred counselling in action*, 2nd ed. London: Sage.

McWilliam, CL, Stewart, M, Brown, JB, McNair, S, Desai, K and Patterson, ML (1996) Creating empowering meaning: an interactive process of promoting health with chronically ill older Canadians. *Health Promotion International*, 12 (2), 111–23.

Mellor-Clark, J, Connell, J, Barkham, M and Cummins, P (2001) Counselling outcomes in primary health care: a CORE system data profile. *European Journal of Psychotherapy & Counselling*, 4 (1): 65–86.

Merleau-Ponty, M (1999) The phenomenology of perception, in Friedman, M (ed) *The worlds of existentialism: a critical reader*. New York: Humanities Books.

Miller, A (1997) *The drama of the gifted child: the search for the true self*. New York: Basic Books.

Miller, S, Duncan, L et al. (2006) Using formal client feedback to improve retention and outcome: making ongoing real-time assessment feasible. *Journal of Brief Therapy* 5 (1): 5–21.

Mitchell, J (ed) (1991) *The selected Melanie Klein*. Harmondsworth: Penguin Books.

Mitchell, J (2002) *Psychoanalysis and feminism*. London: Penguin Books.

Moon, JA (2004) *A handbook of reflective and experiential learning: theory and practice*. London: Routledge.

Moon, JA (2006) *Learning journals: a handbook for reflective practice and professional development*. New York: Routledge.

Muran, JC (ed) (2006) *Dialogues on differences: studies of diversity in the therapeutic relationship*. Washington: APA Books.

Muran, JC and Safran, J (2000) *Negotiating the therapeutic alliance: a relational treatment guide*. New York: Guilford Press.

Nathan, PE, Stuart, SP and Dolan, SL (2000). Research on psychotherapy efficacy and effectiveness: between Scylla and Charybdis? *Psychological Bulletin*, November, 126 (6): 964–81.

NICE (2007) *Management of depression in primary and secondary care*. London: NICE National Institute for Health and Clinical Excellence. Online. Available at www.nice.org.uk/aboutnice/.

Nobus, D (2000) *Jaques Lacan and the Freudian practice of psychoanalysis*. London: Taylor & Francis.

O'Brien, M and Houston, G (2005) *Integrative therapy: a practitioner's guide*. London: Sage.

Ogunfowora, A and Drappeau, M (2008) *A study on the relationship between personality traits and theoretical orientation counselling and psychotherapy research*. New York: Routledge.

Packer, MJ (ed) (2000) *Hermeneutic research on psychotherapy methods: a journal for human science*, Special Issue, Annual Edition. Dallas TX: University of Dallas.

Packer, MJ and Addison, RB (eds) (1989) *Entering the circle: hermeneutic investigation in psychology*. New York: State University of New York.

Paige-Smith, A (2008) *Developing reflective practice in the early years*. Maidenhead: Open University Press.

Park, P (2001) Knowledge and participatory research, in Reason, P and Bradbury, H (eds) *Handbook of action research: participative inquiry and practice*. London: Sage Publications, pp 81–90.

Parker, I (1994) Qualitative research, in Banister, P, Burman, E, Parker, I, Taylor, M and Tindall, C (eds) *Qualitative methods in psychology: a research guide*. Buckingham: Open University Press.

Parker, I (2004) *Qualitative psychology: introducing radical research*. New York: Open University Press.

Paterson, B (2001) Myth of empowerment in chronic illness. *Journal of Advanced Nursing*, 34 (5), 574–81.

Payne, M (1993) *Reading theory: an introduction to Lacan, Derrida, and Kristeva*. DeKalb IL and Oxford: Blackwell.

Pennebaker, JW (1993) Putting stress into words: health, linguistic and therapeutic implications. *Behaviour Research and Therapy*, 31: 539–48.

Philips, D, Penman, D and Linnington, L (1999) *Writing well: creative writing and mental health*. London: Jessica Kingsley.

Polkinghorne, DE (1988) *Narrative knowing and human science*. Albany NY: State University of New York Press.

Portwood, D (2003) Making it work institutionally, in Boud, D and Solomon, N (eds) *Work-based learning: a new higher education*. Buckingham: SRHE Open University Press.

Portwood, D and Costley, C (eds) (2000) *Work based learning and the university: new perspectives and practices*. London: Middlesex University, SEDA.

Proctor, B (1986) Supervision: a co-operative exercise in accountability, in Marken, M and Payne, M (eds) *Enabling and ensuring: supervision in practice*. Leicester: National Youth Bureau.

Rabinow, P (ed) (1991) *The Foucault reader: an introduction to Foucault's thought*. London: Penguin Books.

Rabonowitz, I (ed) (1998) *Inside therapy: illuminating writings about therapists, patients and psychotherapy*. New York: St Martin's Griffin.

Racker, H (2001) *Transference and counter transference*. London: Karnac.

Redmond, B (2006) *Reflection in action: developing reflective practice in health and social services*. Aldershot: Ashgate.

Ricoeur, P (1970) *Freud and philosophy: an essay on interpretation*, Savage, D (trans). New Haven CT and London: Yale University Press.

Ricoeur, P (1998) *Paul Ricoeur: hermeneutics and the human sciences*, Thomson, B (trans and ed). Cambridge: Cambridge University Press.

Riessman, C (1993) *Qualitative research methods*. Sage, University Paper. Newbury Park: Sage.

Robinson, D and Groves, J (2007) *Philosophy: a graphic guide to the history of thinking*. Cambridge: Icon Books.

Roffey-Barentsen, J and Malthouse, R (2009) *Reflective practice in the lifelong learning sector*. Exeter: Learning Matters.

Rogers, C (1961) *A therapist's view of psychotherapy*. London: Constable & Co.

Rogers, C (1995) *A way of being*. New York: Houghton Mifflin.

Rosen, H and Kuelwein, K (eds) (1996) *Constructing realities*. San Francisco CA: Jossey-Bass.

Rowan, J and Jacobs, M (2003) *The therapist's use of self*. Maidenhead: Open University Press.

Ryle, A and Kerr, IB (2000) *Introducing cognitive analytic therapy: principles and practice*. Chichester: Wiley.

Safran, J and Muran, C (1994) Toward a working alliance between research and practice, in Talley, P, Strupp, H and Butler, S (eds) *Psychotherapy research and practice: bridging the gap*. New York: Basic Books.

Saks, ER (1999) Interpreting interpretations: the limits of hermeneutic psychoanalysis. New Haven CT: Yale University.

Sandywell, B (1996) *Reflexivity and the crisis of western reason*. London: Routledge.

Sarup, M (1993) *An introductory guide to post-structuralism and postmodernism*. Harlow: Pearson Education.

Schön, DA (1983) *The reflective practitioner: how professionals think in action*. New York: Basic Books.

Schön, D and Rein, M (1994) *Frame reflection: toward the resolution of intractable policy controversies*. New York: Basic Books.

Schore, AN (2008) The human unconscious: the development of the right brain and its role in early emotional life, in Green, V (ed) *Emotional development in psychoanalysis, attachment theory and neuroscience*. New York: Routledge.

Scruton, R (1996) *Modern philosophy: an introduction and survey*. London: Arrow Books.

Sedgwick, D (1994) *The wounded healer: countertransference from a Jungian perspective*. London: Routledge.

Shawer, L (1998) Notes on the concept of transvaluation, postmodernizing the unconscious. *The American Journal of Psychoanalysis* 8.

Smith, F (1985) *Writing and the write*. London: Heinemann Educational Books.

Sousa, D (2007) From Monet's paintings to Margaret's ducks: divagations on phenomenological research. *Existential Analysis*, 19 (1).

Spinelli, E (2001) The psychotherapist's magic feathers, *Counselling and Psychotherapy Journal*, 12 (6): 6–9.

Stedmon, J and Dallos, R (2009) *Reflective practice in psychotherapy and counselling*. Maidenhead: Open University Press.

Steele, RS (1989) A critical hermeneutics for psychology: beyond positivism to an exploration of textual unconscious, in Packer, MJ and Addison RB (eds) *Entering the circle: hermeneutic investigation in psychology*, New York: State University of New York.

Stern, DN (2004) *The present moment in psychotherapy and everyday life*. New York: Norton.

Strupp, H and Kiesler, D (2006) *The process of psychotherapy: empirical foundations and systems of Analysis*. Chicago IL: Aldine Transaction.

Stuart, C (2006) Using reflexivity in a research methods course: bridging the gap between research and practice in White, S, Fook, J and Gardner, F (eds) *Critical reflection in health and social care*. Maidenhead: Open University Press.

Sussman, MB (1992) *A curious calling: unconscious motivations for practicing psychotherapy*. Lanham MD: Jason Aronson.

Symington, N (1986) *The analytic experience: lectures from the Tavistock*. London: Free Association Books.

Talley, P, Strupp, H and Butler, S (eds) (1994) *Psychotherapy research and practice: bridging the gap*. New York: Basic Books.

Taylor, B (2006) *Reflective practice: a guide for nurses and midwives*. Maidenhead: Open University Press.

Taylor, C (2008) Practising reflexivity: narrative, reflection and the moral order, in White, S, Fook, J and Gardner, F (eds) *Critical reflection in health and social care*. Maidenhead: Open University Press

Tudor-Sandahl, P (2004) *Det omöjliga yrket -om psykoterapi och psykoterapeuter*. Stockholm: Wahlström & Widstrand.

Valerio, P and Mann, D (eds) (2002) *Love and hate: psychoanalytic perspectives*. Hove: Brunner-Routledge.

van Deurzen, E (2009) Existential therapy website. Available at www.existentialpsychotherapy.net/.

Varma, V (ed) (1997) *The needs of counsellors and psychotherapists: emotional, social, physical, professional*. London: Sage.

Wampold, B (2001) *The great psychotherapy debate*. Mahwah NJ: Lawrence Erlbaum Associates.

Weaver, M (2008) Constructivism: some subjective thoughts in a rational world. *The Psychotherapist*, Spring: 1.

Webber, M (2008) *Evidence-based policy and practice in mental health social work*. Exeter: Learning Matters.

White, M (1990) *Narrative means to therapeutic ends*. New York: Norton & Co.

White, S, Fook, J and Gardner, F (2008) *Critical reflection in health and social care*. Maidenhead: Open University Press.

Whitebook, J (1988) Reason and happiness: some psychoanalytic themes in critical theory, in Bernstein, R (ed) *Habermas and modernity*. Oxford: Polity Press.

Wilkinson, H (2009) *The muse as therapist: a new poetic paradigm for psychotherapy*. London: Karnac.

Willis, P (1999) Looking for what it's really like: phenomenology in reflective practice. *Studies in Continuing Education*, 21 (1): 91–112.

Winnicott, DW (1965) *The maturational processes and the facilitating environment*. London: Karnac.

Winnicott, DW (1986) *Home is where we start from*. London: Penguin Books.

Winter, R, Buck, A and Sobiechowska, P (1999) *Professional experience & the investigative imagination: the ART of reflective writing*. London: Routledge.

Wosket, V (2003) *The therapeutic use of self-counselling practice, research and supervision*. Hove: Brunner-Routledge.

Wright, E (2000) *Lacan and postfeminism*. Cambridge: Icon Books.

Yalom, I (1980) *Existential psychotherapy*. New York: Basic Books.

Yalom, I (1991) *Love's executioner: and other tales of psychotherapy*. London and New York: Penguin Books.

Yelloly, M and Henkel, M (2005) *Learning and teaching in social work: towards reflective practice*. London: Jessica Kingsley.

Index